Inch by Inch

GROWING IN LIFE

Compiled by **AIME HUTTON**

CM Publisher
c/o Marketing for Coach, Ltd
Second Floor
6th London Street
W2 1HR London (UK)

www.cm-publisher.com
info@cm-publisher.com

ISBN: 978-0-9929876-0-2

Published in UK, Europe, US and Canada

Book Cover: Csernik Előd

Inside Layout: Csernik Előd

Table of Contents

Foreword

By Sheri Fink

I am so honored to be asked to write the forward for *Inch by Inch: Growing in Life*. If you are a parent looking for inspiration, hope, and encouragement on how your own child will fair in a challenging situation, this thought-provoking book, compiled by Aime Hutton, is your light in the dark tunnel. Or perhaps you experienced something as a child and are feeling stuck, not knowing which way to turn—this book is for you, too! I believe that you can overcome whatever it is that you are going through. You *will* get there.

Inch by Inch is presented to you as a result of sheer determination and persistence from Aime herself. Each curve ball thrown in Aime's direction—from birth into adulthood—has been met with three simple keys that will inspire you to take action and move forward in life

They may seem like small steps, but every step can make a huge impact. The three keys are what helped Aime survive adversities in her life, including being born premature, overcoming bullying, dealing with learning challenges in school, surviving an abusive relationship, and dealing with a stalker. If Aime was able to grow *inch by inch* and thrive each time in her own life, then you can, too!

Aime is a miracle and a true survivor. We are all miracles and have what it takes to not only survive but thrive in our lives. These empowering stories will help you along your journey.

Aime bravely shares her own personal story with you to empower you to keep going. Aime has a big heart, so she has personally invited the other authors to be in the book with her to share their own stories of overcoming childhood adversities.

I continually watch in amazement as Aime works her magic, keeps thriving, and gives the incredible gift of hope to so many families around the world with her first anthology. May it be a source of light in your life, wherever you may be along the journey.

. . . .

Sheri Fink

#1 bestselling, award-winning children's author and founder of "The Whimsical World of Sheri Fink."

Connect with Sheri:

www.SheriFink.com

www.amazon.com/Sheri-Fink/e/B004T9ZJA4

 facebook.com/SheriFinkFan

 twitter.com/Sheri_Fink

. . . .

Acknowledgments

First and foremost, I must thank my parents, Wendy and Barry Hutton. They never gave up on me, especially those first few years of my life. To my sister, Aren Jensen, for her encouragement when we were kids to keep on going in my own life. She stuck up for me in school. And even though she was younger than I, she would challenge anyone who made fun of me on the playground.

The doctors, nurses, and other therapists that helped me grow strong from the neonatal intensive care unit at the Children's Hospital of Eastern Ontario in Ottawa, Ontario—even though they thought the outcome was not going to be positive—they too never gave up.

There are two magical women from England and Spain whom, without them, this anthology would never have happened. Big thanks and gratitude to the duo of Kate Gardner and Christine Marmoy for pushing me outside my box (again) and for telling me to "fly" to create this anthology. And thanks to Christine's team of professional editors, web designers, and book coordinators. They were patient with me as I asked question upon question. They always answered with grace and understanding.

There are seven special women in business that have been there for me since I started my adventure of being an entrepreneur. My Femtor, Jo Dibblee, bestselling author of *Frock Off!*, who took me under her wing and told me she wanted to help me grow and glow. Jo is a special woman in my life who brought me into eWomen Network when she was executive managing director of Calgary for the Chapter. She saw me when I was broken, and that one sentence, "I believe in YOU," has made all the difference.

Karen Luniw, CEO of Attract More Now and bestselling author of *A Year of Wow!,* inspired me to ask, "What else is possible?" She taught me to stretch outside my box three years ago.

Karen Klassen, founder of Women Embracing Brilliance and bestselling author of *The Freedom Frequency*, keeps reminding me that my brilliance is meant to shine and light others in their own dark time.

The dynamic Debra Kasowski and Charmaine Hammond, bestselling authors of *GPS Your Best Life*, have both been amazing at teaching me to ask for help, in a number of different situations. They help me to remember to dream big and keep moving forward toward my dreams.

And finally, but certainly not least, from these seven angels in my business life are the writing queens, Farhana Dhalla and Laura Crowe. Farhana is a bestselling author of *Thank You for Leaving Me* and Laura is my first ever editor for a book I took part in for her called *Take Flight: True Stories of How Dreams Shape Our Lives*. Both of these women got me into the writing world to be published so I could share my story with others. It was these ladies who first told me that you never know who you will help by sharing your own story with others in a book.

Special thanks and much gratitude to Colleen Doey-Kelba and her amazing husband, Grant Kelba. For opening their doors at their retreat space for me to come and heal from the hospital procedure, and where most of my writing took place for this anthology for you. I was able to get away from the city for short periods of time to heal, write, and concentrate on ME.

Lastly, the one person I can't forget to thank is my business mastermind partner Carrie-Ann Barron (founder of Solvo Coaching, and international bestselling author of *The Missing Piece: A Transformational Journey)*. Connecting with Carrie-Ann has been amazing—we push and encourage each other to go higher in business. And Carrie-Ann, your grace, laughter, and tenacity with me in the hospital and the following days after have been such a blessing to my spirit.

Most importantly, this anthology couldn't be in your hands if it wasn't for all the amazing authors who took a risk and shared their story with you. The authors are remarkable, brave, and have been a joy to work with. Thank YOU, everyone!

Inch by Inch

Introduction

Everyone on earth goes through challenges—things they face in their lives that they have to learn, overcome, and achieve. Just last year, for example, I chose to overcome my fear of writing and went on to be published in my second internationally-collaborated book, called *The Missing Piece: A Transformational Journey*, compiled by Kate Gardner. *The Missing Piece* was a book of women sharing stories about overcoming adversity, mostly as adults. From domestic abuse, cancer, or the loss of a child, these stories made an impact on the readers worldwide.

Being in *The Missing Piece: A Transformational Journey* got me thinking. Children overcome adversity as well as adults. Kate encouraged me to put my own anthology out into the world. I have a passion for empowering children. This put a spark in me to search and find parents and professionals who could share a story about children overcoming adversity. In the middle of November in 2013 I saw an International Preemie Day poster at a local children's hospital. International Preemie Day celebrates babies around the world who were born premature and lived. This cemented my idea of creating the book to give hope and inspiration to families right now who are scared that their baby will not live. When I was born in 1976, there weren't any inspirational books for my parents to read while they were sitting in the neonatal intensive care unit. They had family and each other. They hadn't met anyone who had a baby who went through what I did as a baby. Kate agreed that children also experience adversity and loved the idea of this book.

When a child is overcoming a challenge, the whole family is affected and involved. The parents want the best possible outcome for their baby. They want their son or daughter to laugh and play with the other kids, not stuck in a hospital bed.

Parents have hopes and dreams for their children. But when the doctor tells them they have a sick baby, or a baby born with a disability, it's a whole different ballgame. They just want their baby to *live*.

When parents find out that their child has learning difficulties, or is the target of bullying, or some other obstacle, some parents may look for inspiration from children who have been where their son/daughter is right now. They want their child to be happy and achieve their dreams. Some children endure intense situations at a young age and are scarred for life. How did the children overcome those situations? What you will find in these pages will inspire you, give you hope, and yes, you may shed a few tears, as well.

Inch by Inch: Growing in Life was created just like that: inch by inch, step by step. Rome wasn't built overnight. Neither was this book. I never gave up though. I kept going. I used my network and reached out to connections around the world who might know of someone with a story to share about overcoming adversity as a child. I asked for help from others to create this anthology and that was key in bringing it to life for you to read today.

As the story ideas from people came in, I was blown away by everyone's courage to step up and speak about what they went through, or what the child they know went through. Each author in this book is so brave, sharing a personal piece of them with you, the reader, to help you move forward and grow in your own life, as well as helping your own family, who might be experiencing difficulty. Each author will provide you with tools and tips on how to grow in your own life.

Halfway through putting this anthology together, I found myself in the hospital. I live with a hormone imbalance, and my specialist wanted to try something new. Going through a procedure in the hospital was minor, and it had the potential to either create a better or worse situation. I took a risk, trusted the doctor, and went ahead with the procedure.

While taking a few days to heal after the procedure, I thought about many things. I retreated out to the foothills of the Rocky Mountains here in Alberta. I got to thinking about all those who are sitting in the hospital with their baby. Their worries and fears about how their babies will survive. And what problems will come of their baby being born with complications. I've never experienced the worrying feeling of holding my baby in my arms. For I've never had children of my own. Yet what I do know is that all children are miracles and deserve the best life possible. Yes, many struggle and fight to live, experience unthinkable trauma, and endure some of the most painful moments in their physical body. They will overcome it, inch by inch. May this book be a source of inspiration, hope, and celebration for you! If the children you read about in this anthology did it, so can you!

Each author you meet is sharing with you a remarkable story of pushing past the adversity, rising above their stories, to help you do the same. Some stories will have you may possibly have you teary eyed and cheering, all at the same time. The children you'll meet in the stories are remarkable and brave.

Together, we can create a change for the better, to give hope to others who are experiencing a challenge or adversity. I once heard that it takes a village to raise a child, and this book will be a source of community for you to help raise your own child to grow and thrive.

One thing I love to do is give back. And this time it's all about building a community to give back. You have bought this book, or it was gifted to you by a friend or family member. Because the book was purchased on Amazon, part of the proceeds will be going to the neonatal intensive care unit at the Children's Hospital of Eastern Ontario, to give them support because they help so many sick and fragile children. If it wasn't for the team of doctors there, I might not be here today to share my own story of hope with others. You can find out more about CHEO here: www.cheo.on.ca

I encourage and invite you to connect with the authors and myself after you have read the stories. We want to help you grow, *inch by inch*, in your own life. If we did it, so can YOU!

Here's to you growing in your own life and inspiring your family to do the same!

Aime Hutton
Empowerment Leader
Two-time international bestselling author
Canadian Ambassador for
Freedom & Empowerment Campaign

Aime Hutton

Hailing from Calgary, Alberta, Canada, Aime is a true survivor. Being born three months early was just the start of her struggles she had to overcome in her life. Aime is now an empowerment leader, helping tween and teen girls believe in themselves when they think no one does. She is also a two-time international bestselling author and Canadian ambassador for the Freedom & Empowerment Campaign, a global campaign dealing with domestic abuse and dating violence, for which she won the International Ambassador of the Year for 2013.

Contacts/social media:

www.inchbyinchempowerment.com

www.freedomandempowerment.com

✉ **aime@inchbyinchempowerment.com**

f **facebook.com/pages/Inch-by-Inch-Empowerment/411465042319765**

🐦 **twitter.com/IBIEmpowerment**

▶ **youtube.com/user/dracof24**

in **ca.linkedin.com/pub/aime-hutton/34/b4b/b76/**

CHAPTER 1

WILL SHE LIVE?

By Aime Hutton

I've lost count of the number of times people have asked me, "How are you alive?" with wide-eyed expressions. Many times, people look at me and shake their heads. It's a will and a drive from deep within that pushes me forward every time I'm up against a wall. How is it that I am alive today in 2014 as an internationally published author, empowerment leader, and a Canadian ambassador for a global campaign about domestic violence and dating abuse? Let me back up and share with you the story of how I came into this world.

The year was 1976; it was fall in Ottawa, Ontario. The trees were changing to vibrant reds, crisp oranges, and luscious yellows. Outside, it was a beautiful sunny fall day. However, inside Riverside Hospital, in the maternity ward, it wasn't so cheery. A first-time mother had just given birth to her daughter. With a furrowed brow, the doctors said to this new mother and father, "Your daughter is very sick. She might not survive the night. Being born three months early, her weight of one pound twelve ounces is the smallest we've seen here. We're going to transfer her to a new children's hospital that just opened up not too far from here, which has a team ready who specialize in cases like this."

My mum gripped my dad's hands, and with tears welling in her eyes, asked the doctor, "What's wrong with our daughter? Will she live?"

As if the doctor had heard this a million times before, he sighed and replied, "The first twenty-four hours are critical. She is in grave danger of not surviving. If she does live, she will always be small and petite."

"She looks like a drowned, shriveled-up baby rat!" my dad exclaimed in a panic. My dad huffed in a worried state, looking at me in the glass-enclosed isolette with wires, IV's, and various machines hooked up around it. The day nurse came in and smiled at my father. "Your daughter is a little fighter. There were a few times overnight that we had to remind her to breathe. That's what this machine is for," the nurse said, pointing to one of the machines with lots of numbers and lights on it, a long tube stretching into the isolette near my tiny head. The doctor joined my dad and nurse by that time, adding, "We're not out of the woods yet, Mr. Hutton. Your daughter will need special treatment and monitoring for a few months, maybe even years."

The doctor was right. It did take time for me to grow strong and big enough to go home. There were setbacks— I wasn't eating enough, I needed to be reminded to breathe, and I developed a few serious blood infections and some infections in my throat and stomach. Yet little by little, I grew stronger.

There were many nights that I was alone in the NICU at the Children's Hospital of Eastern Ontario, only the sounds of beeps and little squawks—no loving voices from family. It was up to me to fight to live at that moment. There was a will and drive to remain alive.

"She's not walking yet!" Mum was talking on the phone to one of the therapists. I was nearly one and a half years old and still not walking. Other things had developed slowly too, like my speech—it hadn't developed as a normal full-term baby's would have. "Keep doing the mobility exercises with her, Mrs. Hutton. She will walk with help from you both."

The therapist suggested I take swimming lessons to help with muscle strength and dance to help with coordination and balance. I'm pretty sure I took to water very easy, as my parents were both lifeguards when they were younger and they'd put me in the water often as a baby.

Fast forward to 1980, when my sister was born. The doctor's pulled my father aside and said their new baby, my sister Aren, was going to potentially have many problems and struggles ahead. She was also a preemie and very small. Grinning at the doctor, my dad pointed to a photo in his wallet of me at four years old and said, "Tell me something new doctor. This is my older daughter, Aime. She wasn't supposed to live back in 1976 and she was also small like her sister, smaller even. Her doctor also gave her twenty-four hours to live. Now she's dancing and playing like any other four-year-old little girl should."

I did have some mobility issues growing up though and returned to the hospital many times for specialty treatments and assessments. "She may have polio," one doctor said to my parents. But ultimately, these doctors concluded I didn't have polio simply by observing the way I walked and stood, and they looked again at the x-rays that showed I was born with my left hip out of place. When extremely tired, I walked with a limp, but to keep me active and moving would help strengthen my muscles around my hip joint.

I also had challenges in school. Teachers noticed I was struggling with math, spelling, and comprehension. I was tested for a number of academic abilities. The doctors in those academic fields said I was a slow learner and would always have difficulty in school. They said I needed extra help in academic core subjects (math and English). So I was held back in third grade. I was taken out of the class for extra tutoring help in math and English. I was even going to a different class for English, to get help.

"Wendy and Barry, Aime needs extra help, and we're not sure if her teacher can fully be there to help her through the day. We suggest she be placed in a separate class and get the attention and help that she needs to fully complete her schooling." The school guidance counselor, principal, and teacher for my third grade year were meeting with my parents. Mum and Dad looked back at the school guidance counselor, and with a very commanding voice, my father said, and "Aime will not be going into any special class fulltime. She will continue in her grade where she is and stay there with her peers. Yes, Aime has been through a lot in her life already; putting her in a special class fulltime will dampen her spirit and not challenge her to do her best always. Keep giving her help, and extra homework—we will work with her at home, too." That is what happened. I had extra help in the core studies of math and English. My parents did agree to have me held back a year to redo grade three so I could get extra help and catch up on my skills. I can remember nights of tears at the kitchen table with spelling and math homework, struggling for hours to get through it all. Yet I did it. I graduated from the school without being in a special class fulltime. I was even nominated as the "Most Improved Student" in my graduating year of grade eight.

There are three tips that I want to give to you on how you can get through any situation. Subconsciously, it's how I got through those first few years of my life, and even now as an adult, it's how I have overcome all the challenges in my life. It takes a team to make dreams come true.

- **Put one foot in front of the other.** No matter how big or small the step is. Just keep moving forward. Take a step towards your goals and your dreams. Encourage your children to create goals and help them take steps to move toward them. I had chosen to do that as a baby—if I wanted to live, I had to keep going no matter what.

- **Believe in yourself.** If I didn't have the will and the fight in me as a preemie baby, I wouldn't be here today. I can only imagine those quiet lonely nights the first few months of my life, fighting to live. I could have given up even then. Yet I didn't. I believed in me.

- **Let others help you.** Ask for help. People can't read your mind either. I had to let the nurses and doctors help me. And my parents both had to ask for help for me and then let the doctors and specialists help me to grow. It takes team work to make the dream work. People will want to help you. Let them!

Inch by Inch

16

Lil Lezarre

Lil and her fifteen-year-old daughter, Shae, have been through some tough times, including fleeing from domestic abuse and alienation. They now have the best mother/daughter relationship ever. Sharing a mixed relationship of love, honesty, and humor, they connect more than ever. They share their advice and perspectives to help offer hope for other parent/child relationships.

✉ **lil@lilspbf.ca**

✉ **shaem08@hotmail.com**

f **Lily Lezarre; Shae Masse**

> Lil and I met on another book project. To have her be a part of this anthology is awesome. Lil is grace, determination, and brilliance all in one. Thank YOU, Lil, for being in this book project!
>
> ~ **Aime Hutton**

CHAPTER 2

MOM, I KNOW I CAN TELL YOU ANYTHING

By Lil Lezarre

Not something I experienced as a child, but because of that, it was always my priority with my kids. My mom was a very religious and controlling person, and I never had the freedom to set my own boundaries. So, at sixteen years old, I ran away from home…right into another controlling relationship. Twenty-two years and three children later, I finally found the courage and support network I needed to leave: I was thirty-nine years old and only then was I able to work on my boundaries and discover myself.

When I left with my children, they were just four, six, and eight years old. Life at the shelter and in subsidized housing was very stressful. I worked hard to control my emotions and stop yelling, always making it a priority that they could tell me anything. The purpose of my chapter is to show parents the importance of allowing kids to be themselves and allowing them to realize their own boundaries.

My ex is a very manipulative man and our children were easy targets. Both sons returned to live with their dad when they were ten. Heartbreakingly, living with their dad meant little to none or only negative contact with me. When Shae was twelve, she lived with her dad for almost a year and came back to me when she was thirteen. It had taken years and many, many tears to resign myself to the boys being gone from my life, and that year, with no Shae, was the only time I experienced depression.

In the wake of Shae's choice to go live with her dad, I made it clear my door was always open if and when she decided to move back. It turned out living with her dad was a good thing, as she experienced firsthand what it is like to be forced to be dishonest. Now when she comes back from a visit, she explains how uncomfortable she is when hearing his tall tales and lies because she is aware of her boundaries.

Honesty is huge to me. Living the first thirty-nine years of my life having to lie for survival, first with my mom and then with my ex for fear of punishment or repercussions, I relish the fact that now I have the freedom to say what's on mind and express my feelings. I also appreciate that I have a partner, Michael, who shares the same values as I do. This gives Shae two adults in our home with whom she can share whatever she wants to without fear of any kind.

Today, I am thrilled to have a loving connection with the boys again, and Shae and I have the most amazing relationship I could imagine. I'm so proud of how far she's come in the past three years. She really has come into her own person.

How was our relationship repaired and revitalized?

It began with my acceptance that we are 100 percent responsible for our reaction to every situation; a person must acquire the tools to react appropriately. I worked on myself for years with counselors and coaches.

- Always reflect back to when you were your child's age. Put yourself in your child's position and your child's perspective, always honor their view (no matter how unrealistic or uniformed it is from an adult perspective). Remember being scared of the closet or dark places?

- Listen to their side with 100 percent of your attention. If they have something to say about you, don't take it personally. How can they be totally honest with you if they have to first think how to say it so your emotions are not triggered? Remember, your child has probably not yet developed the vocabulary or the emotional capacity to understand and convey all the nuances of their concerns.

- If they come to you at a bad time, set a time that's good and follow through. If they know they can count on your word, they will also be flexible.

- If they have something to say that they know will elicit a strong response, ask them to give you a "warning" so you can calm down before the conversation and make a conscientious effort to have a decent conversation with them.

- Respect is a two-way street—we automatically expect it from our kids but you have to set the example by respecting them. It can start as simply as just never walking in to their bedroom when they're in it, always knocking first, and asking if it's OK to come in.

- Let them say their side first with no interruptions. Calm conversations go a long way and once they've gotten it off their chest, they're more likely to be open to listening to your side and advice.

I found this last piece of advice—no interruptions—to be very hard, especially whenever I didn't agree with Shae. However, I saw the difference firsthand when we were in a counseling session.

Our dog, Rolo, was hit by a car when Michael took him off his leash. Shae was so furious with Michael and accused him of killing Rolo. He was devastated by the accident too, but there was no talking to her—conversations always blew up into a fight. As Shae was talking to the counselor, I wanted to butt in and say, "That's not how it is!" but after the counselor acknowledged Shae's feelings repeatedly, she was open to seeing that Michael didn't do that on purpose and a different Shae walked out of that session. All she needed was her feelings validated first.

Kids do need boundaries and consequences for their actions. For example, Michael and I cut our summer vacation short because Shae would throw a tantrum when she didn't get her way. One day when she didn't want to sleep on the pull-out couch in the living room at the condo, Shae screamed at the top of her lungs, calling me names and saying that I love Michael more than her and that I do everything for Michael and nothing for her. As a consequence, I stopped doing her laundry, chauffeuring her around (she always had bus tickets), and making her lunches (there was never a shortage of food in the fridge). She soon realized how much I did for her, and to this day, I don't do her laundry.

I support Shae in everything she wants to do. Shae and her friend make jewelry and I give them half my table at trade shows to sell their goods. I was very surprised how important it was to her when I made her business cards—she thought that was the coolest thing, but I had seen it as just a convenience. You may never know how each small gesture of respect for your child's interests will impact your relationship.

I will always support my kids in their decisions. I will give them advice if I don't agree with it and my reasons for that, but the final decision is theirs (unless their safety is at risk, then there has to be compromise to remove the risk). Likewise, I will always be there to support them when they realize the outcome—good or bad. That's how we get experience—by learning from our mistakes. They have to know you will be there for them no matter what. Respect them and their decisions and in return, they respect you—what more could you want as a parent?

SHAE'S HALF

My mom has shown me many important lessons and strategies in life. We have bonded and have the strongest relationship we have ever had because of the hard times we've gone through together. There are three types of parents: the ones who don't care what choices their children make, aren't there for them, and let them do whatever they want. Then there are the overprotective parents who make their children's choices for them, don't give their kids any space, and answer their questions for them. In between those two are parents like my mom. She lets me make my own decisions—unless there is a chance of harm or danger. At home, I am never lonely, I always have someone to talk to and confide in. Honesty is also a large role in our house. I think these aspects are very important for a thriving family. Parents need to realize that their children have their own lives and sometimes need space. You also need to realize that we are not adults, we require help sometimes. If your child doesn't do as well as you expect them to do in school, help them, don't criticize or make them feel bad. Friends are also extremely important in anybody's life. If you don't agree with your child's friends, tell them, don't exempt them from hanging out with their friends.

Alara Payten

Alara Payten combines spiritual intuition and sacred heart wisdom to help women make peace with their past, their bodies, and their lives, so they can live powerfully in the now and create the deeply fulfilling lives they deserve.

Twenty-four years of practice as a physical therapist, (under the name Brenda Hope Gibbs), supports her expertise as an inner journey specialist, energy alchemist, and Community Mother Drum Portal Journey guide.

Her work frees women who are sick and tired of being prisoners of their own past. She compassionately guides each woman to reclaim their personal power, their authentic voice, and their empowered choice.

www.alarapayten.com

✉ **alara@alarapayten.com**

f **facebook.com/AlaraPayten**

🐦 **twitter.com/AlaraPayten**

in **ca.linkedin.com/pub/alara-payten/80/a4a/b99/**

> Alara is a true gem. Her wisdom and love for others seeps through everything she does. I am so grateful and blessed to have YOU, Alara, be a part of this book!
>
> ~ **Aime Hutton**

23

CHAPTER 3

IT'S NEVER TOO LATE TO HEAL OUR PAST!

By Alara Payten

Yes, it's true! I have proof that it's never too late to heal our past. Never too late to make peace with that past: a peace that sets us free to live powerfully in the ever-present now and lays the foundation for creating a deeply fulfilling life.

My first proof came after the death of my father. For two years, I ran away from my grief. I kept myself obsessively busy so I didn't have the time or energy to deal with my overwhelming emotions.

I was a walking time bomb! I was unpredictable and became verbally and emotionally abusive to my children and my husband. My marriage was stressed to the max.

I was abruptly awakened to the need to get help when my husband looked at me one night and asked, "Do you want a divorce?"

We chose to see a relationship therapist together. It quickly became evident that the most pressing need was for me to heal the unresolved issues around my father's death. So I started my grief-healing journey through the doorway of individual counseling sessions.

One of the main tools we used was roleplaying. I imagined my deceased father sitting in a chair across from me. I shared my feelings with him as honestly as I could. I imagined him listening fully and compassionately to my every word.

Then, I physically moved to "my father's" chair and pretended that *I was* my father. I spoke as my father would to his daughter, as though "she" were sitting in the chair across from me. I shared as fully and completely as I could as the father. I switched roles many times. It was surprisingly easy to play pretend, as I had often done as a child.

Through this process, I owned the crushing guilt that I was dragging along in life, guilt from wishing in childhood that my father would just drop dead. Guilt that I had wished for a different father, one who didn't hide in the basement with his debilitating depression. A father who wasn't deeply scarred from serving on the European front lines during World War II.

Over time, I worked through the seething anger that was poisoning me. I released the life-sucking sadness that was paralyzing my life. A deep, profound change occurred in me the day I gave away the pain I'd carried on my father's behalf since early childhood.

It was amazing how committed I was to holding onto my father's pain, how reluctant I was to give up that heavy burden. It had become a part of my identity. I agreed to release it only after he convinced me that he was now ready, willing, and able to carry all of his own pain and hurts. He showed me how his expanded viewpoint from the spirit realm allowed him to embrace the value of the life he had lived and the wisdom gained through that journey.

I came to peace with that part of my past, although the other person was not even in the room with me. Indeed, he was not even on the planet with me.

The second experience that proved to me it's never too late to heal our past happened six months before my fortieth birthday. I remember it clearly. I was visiting my widowed mother. She was visibly upset but reluctant to share why. After some prodding from me, she spoke these words: "[Your cousin] says that Grandpa sexually abused her."

As my mother shared more details about what my cousin had experienced, my body began to shake and I started to cry. I felt an excruciating sadness for our family as I witnessed my mother's shock, disbelief, and pain at the possibility that her own father had been a child molester. Somehow I sensed that my cousin's words were true.

My grandfather had died when I was twenty-two, a month after my wedding. Since childhood, I remembered that he had fondled children

—including me—through their clothing when other adults weren't in the room but I'd never consciously labeled that as sexual abuse.

Over the following weeks, I heard my mother's words swirling around in my head. I became overwrought with emotion and panic attacks. I had always experienced varying degrees of anxiety and depression for as long as I could remember. Now my life was overtaken by the aftermath of those fateful words from my cousin.

By the time my fortieth birthday came around in February, I was suffocating in a deep pit of depression. My system was under so much stress that I developed pneumonia. After the repeated force of coughing myself to exhaustion, I ruptured a disc in my neck, adding the load of physical pain and weakness caused by the disc protrusion.

I felt crushed by life. I had suicidal thoughts as my desperation grew. Finally, I was literally brought to my knees by the weight of my pain. Somehow in that surrender, I found the courage to make a phone call to a counseling center.

I promised myself that I wouldn't cry during the call. Ha! I managed to keep that promise for all of five seconds. The tears started and wouldn't stop. I apologized a dozen times to the intake woman asking questions on the other end of the line. She remained calm, compassionate, and unphased by my overflowing emotions.

As the day of the first appointment approached, my sense of dread grew. What was I going to find out that I didn't want to know?

The day finally arrived and I sat in the appointment room with the social worker assigned to me. I immediately felt wrapped in the warmth of her compassionate, professional manner, and we bonded with amazing ease. I allowed her to guide me through the doorway of discovery and into the deep recesses of my unconscious mind where I had buried the memories of sexual assaults by my grandfather.

She skillfully found a way through the minefield of terrifying and overwhelming memories that even included a near-death experience. Repressed memories that had held me hostage for thirty-five years were set free.

She and the other supporters that followed guided me in the healing of my past and the liberation of my life. I moved from barely surviving to the infinite possibilities available in thriving.

The third experience that proved to me that it's never too late to heal our past started when I was fifty-one. My beloved mother had the onset of life-threatening health challenges. Over the course of the next three years, she (and those who loved her) rode the ultra-wild emotional and physical rollercoaster-from-hell as she faced her mortality.

Early on, I sensed she was not going to have a physical healing of the rare form of intestinal blockage and cancer that had developed; rather, she would have the opportunity for deep relationship healings.

And that's what she got. It was my privilege and honor to facilitate numerous inner-child healing sessions for my mum. To guide her through the healing opportunities that she had been avoiding for years, sometimes decades.

Through her courage and choice, my mother came to find peace about her unresolved childhood wounds that transcended all human understanding.

By the time I stood at her head, as she took her last breath at the age of eighty, my mum had healed the relationships she needed to heal, said what she needed to say, and heard what she needed to hear.

A few days before her passing, Mum shared with my dear friend that she was grateful for the numerous opportunities God had given her to make peace with her past. While she was tired of the unrelenting pain, she was no longer afraid to die. She was now ready join her husband in heaven.

The courage my mother showed in her seventies and her willingness to walk through the fires of healing and transformation of her childhood wounds has given me even more proof that it is indeed never too late for anyone to heal their past.

I feel so blessed that I am no longer addicted to the victimhood and drama of my past. I have gathered many priceless treasures along my journey of self-discovery and recovery, and I know that if I can do it, others can too.

If you have a hurt from your past that is stopping you from living your life powerfully now, I urge you to reach out and find the people and methods that will help *you* to bring peace to *your* past. You are not alone! You can do it!

Vivian Sollows

I am most proud of being a mom to three beautiful children. I am a creative entrepreneur with big dreams. My projects include a healthy dry mix you add to your favorite recipe called OH!mega Meal Boost, an accessible music program with no criteria to participate no matter age or type of disability, recording my songs, and obtaining a foot pedal magnifier to play classical guitar again.

OH!mega Meal Boost

📞 **613-247-1917**

✉ **viviansollows@gmail.com**

▶ **youtube.com/vividarlingmusicproject**

Vivian and I met through a mutual friend on Facebook. She was the first to sign on for the project. Thank YOU, Vivian, for your belief in me from the start and for being in this book!

~ Aime Hutton

CHAPTER 4

MORE TO LIFE THAN YOU CAN SEE

By Vivian Sollows

I was five years old when I rode my bike into a chain link fence on a cloudy day. This is how my parents found out there was something wrong with my eyes. I became so light sensitive I wouldn't go outside to play. My vision slowly worsened over time from 50/20 to 200/20 and now 400/20. This means what a person sees with healthy vision at 400 feet, I can only see at 20 feet in ideal lighting conditions. Add into the equation extreme light sensitivity and color deficiency— there are times I see only a sheet of gray, like trying to see through a tinted window. On a sunny day in the summer, I see shadows to know there's a step or a building. Headaches occur daily and when they're really severe, they cause my vision to fluctuate. When someone with visual impairments experiences vision changes based on their environment, misunderstandings arise and people often question your actions. If you don't self-identify by using a white cane, many people think you're on drugs or mentally ill. As I've grown through life experiences, I've found I must look for creative adaptive solutions to accomplish what I want to do and I'm no longer ashamed of using any tool necessary.

Even though my vision has been a barrier in my development, the negative attitude of others has been more of burden. Throughout grade school, I was a good student who received all A's, except in gym, but it was hard to make friends. Every year, I was teased about being the four-eyed fat girl. The only time I had a friend was near the end of the school year when a new girl arrived, but by next September, she would no longer be interested in being my friend. In high school, girls shunned me and boys bullied me because I was significantly overweight. By the end of tenth grade, I was starting to excel at playing tenor saxophone; music became my solace. My vision drastically worsened, and I couldn't see to read the music and hold the saxophone. I couldn't keep up with the course load. I was exhausted by four o'clock every day, so I wasn't capable of doing any more work. I couldn't take notes off the board or a projector. Students went all different directions for eight courses so there was no one student I could ask for notes. I was struggling just to follow by ear, a new skill I needed to learn. Teachers told me I was lazy and believed I was using my vision as an excuse not to do the work. The guidance counselors told me they saw no future in education for me. Even my mother told me, "If it's too hard, just don't do it." I dropped out of school in eleventh grade at age fifteen, with very little self-worth, since my innate personality was introverted and harsh criticism was difficult to take.

At this time, my father started to drive me to look for someone suitable to marry without my mother's knowledge. I did marry at age eighteen to a man I met who was twenty-two. At first I was happy. I studied classical guitar because I could bring the papers closer to my face than I could with a saxophone. I went back to a term school and took night classes for adults. I finished with good marks but didn't attend my graduation ceremony—neither my parents nor husband supported my achievement. The following year, I found out I'd made the honor roll when a classmate I saw at the mall asked me why I didn't attend graduation. I had so little confidence I actually thought most people did just as well I had—why would I receive an award? I left Ottawa at twenty-one years old to live in a new town where my husband had friends and an opportunity to go to college. I thought it would work out because it was someplace new and exciting.

I took menial jobs for a few years and then landed work at an accounting firm where I became an expert in New Views accounting systems. I was offered a chance to become a partner managing operations. I thrived and felt satisfaction with the purpose of helping business owners with their taxes. I thought I could run a business of my own so I started a large print bookstore. I submerged myself in work because my marriage was failing. Then my mother was diagnosed with lung cancer and I decided to move back to Ottawa to take care of her. During this time, my mother told me she thought I would stay home and take care of her all of my life—that I'd never have a relationship, a job, and definitely not children. She was embarrassed because I was overweight. She never acknowledged any of my accomplishments and didn't know me. I was deeply hurt.

I yearned to have a normal life with a career, a relationship, children, and my own little house. I'd battled with feeling inferior all my life. I felt abandoned and forgotten by God. After my mother died, I felt I no longer had to prove anything. I couldn't stay with my husband—I couldn't change or help him, although I gave him many chances. I wanted to forget reality so I acted out, was reckless, and had an affair with a man from Cuba I met on vacation. To my amazement, our relationship continued several months after the trip. He was six feet tall and handsome—a real ladies man—but I knew it wasn't serious for him. Still, it felt good to be wanted and to feel passion for a time. Then I became pregnant and had a little girl. When my daughter was six months old, I met and started dating the father of my two boys and we've been together since. I believe children need two parents and I wanted a stable relationship.

I chose to have children, not knowing my third child would be born with serious health issues, which only compounded the financial issues in my family. There are many therapies my son needs, like speech pathology, which is not considered a medical necessity. It's not covered under government health programs, even though he has a cleft palate. My determination to figure out how to do things for myself because of my vision problems provided me with the ability to advocate for my son. He gave me inspiration to go back to the dream of having my own business. He required care 24/7, so I needed to make money at home. I designed a recycle bin on wheels and a monkey toy but both needed more capital to produce. I tried setting up home catering for healthy baked goods, since I am a gifted baker, and that led to the development of a new health food product I call OH!mega Meal Boost. One day, my daughter (twelve years old) and son (seven years old) were fighting over who got more bran buds on their yogurt parfait—not the blueberries or the chocolate chips, as I would have expected. I was sad my youngest son couldn't enjoy the treat. I started to experiment with grinding ingredients and researching nutrition. The mix is easy to chew, tastes great, and provides high protein, fiber, and essential fatty acids. It can be added to many of your favorite recipes without nutritional values being degraded when heated. I have been seriously pursuing creating a sustainable business, taking courses with a business mentor.

My love for music has always remained. I stopped playing guitar due to loss of vision but also had no time since my youngest was always sick, but I continued singing every day. I have written many songs I believe people need to hear. I included the words to one of them below. I aspire to create an accessible music program to allow others to experience the healing power of music. Go to youtube.com for Vividarling Music Project and OH!mega Meal Boost: viviansollows@gmail.com

"MORE TO LIFE"

Lay down, come and lay down here
Close your eyes, forget your fears
Let me wipe away your tears
So you can hold on to your honor
Hold on to your dreams
Sometimes you just want to give in
You don't know where to begin
My friend, let me tell you this
Hold on to your dreams and you'll be blessed

There's more to life than you can see
It all comes down to what you believe
I know I've done my very best
It's time to let go of all the rest
So I can hold on to my honor
And hold on to my dreams

I no longer see that much
I rely on my sense of touch
I listen close, to everything
Proud of myself 'cause I held on to my dreams
Yeah there's more to life than you can see.

Inch by **Inch**

Donna Davis

Although there are many ways to heal (most of them serious and intense), my favorite way is through laughter and fun. Being an educator and teacher for over thirty years has allowed my students and me this blessed luxury.

I love experiencing the joy of life. Celebrating the journeys of those around me as I continue to live, love, laugh, and heal myself. (It's not always fun playing in the sandbox alone).

I enjoy artsy crafty things including sewing, crocheting, vision boarding, coloring, and play of all types. (I even run well with scissors!)

Contacts:

 (201) 306-0975

 ddavis350@yahoo.com

Donna and I met via Val (who is also in this book). Donna, thank YOU for being in this book with us. Your story is going to help others around the world!

~ Aime Hutton

CHAPTER 5

...BUTT FIRST!

By Donna Davis

On a hot summer day, she decides it's time, time to come into this world... butt first.

For some reason, I decided to arrive a month early...with a statement! After coming down the birth canal, I changed my mind, went back up, flipped all around, and THEN came out...butt first. This would be a pattern that I continued repeating well into my forties.

My lips were blue, I had pneumonia, my leg stuck way up in the air, and I was given seventy-two hours to live. What a way to start a life!

Little did I know exactly what a ride this life would turn out to be. It was later when I realized how angry I was and that my silent motto turned out to be: "I came into this world butt first and now everyone can kiss my a**!" My grand entrance attested to that fact.

I was angry at the world. I was angry at God.

Why did my parents have to split? Dad was gone and mom gave up. How can a four year old possibly manage by herself when mommy is passed out and won't wake up to take care of her? "I want my mommy! WHY won't she love me? Can't you see I need my mommy? I can only see my dad on Saturdays?" I felt helpless and hopeless — was I doomed to feel this way forever?

Why did that gang have to target me? Was I easy prey? Was it because I always seemed or felt alone and vulnerable? Why did they have to wait outside to terrorize me as soon as I walked out of the house? Sometimes they would yell, laugh, and mock me whenever I stayed in the house for days on end. Didn't they have better things to do than to torment me? This world seemed so threatening and horrible. Would I ever feel safe? Could I ever relax?

Why did I have to be molested at age ten? You were a close family friend, didn't you know better? Weren't you the adult!? There was no one to trust or count on. I thought my life was just a waste, that there must not be any happiness anywhere. I felt abandoned and ashamed. Was everyone this miserable?

Why was that man such a pervert when I was sixteen? I was hired to be a house cleaner, not a personal servant. I didn't want you to watch me as I washed the floor. No, I didn't want to rub that lotion on your back, and no, I was NOT looking for a sugar daddy! What the hell does that mean anyway? Did life get better than this?

Why were there so many horrific, unspeakable events that kept presenting and repeating themselves throughout my life? Was I doomed to a life of utter misery and depression? Was it possible to fix all the broken parts, all the shattered pieces?

How did I get on that roller coaster? Why were there no seatbelts? Safety harnesses? Where the hell were the brakes? Stop this ride I want to get off!

We get busy being busy. Distracted by whatever means possible to keep the thoughts, feelings, and memories at bay. To numb out. To check out. To get so involved with helping or saving anybody— everybody else. We think it's too painful to heal. Won't it be just as miserable or worse to relive it all over again by talking about it? By feeling those horrible feelings? The answer is no. The fact is, the worse thing already happened. Regardless of why or how. We owe it to ourselves to heal. To reach out, to reach up to a helping hand extended to help guide us on our path. A peaceful path full of promise and joy, if we only but dare to allow it. We continuously replay the tapes in our heads of the event(s) anyway. Why not dare to find a way to heal? To have hope? To no longer be the victim? To stand up by ourselves and for ourselves.

In life, we tend to put others first, even before our own healing and growth.

I'll get some help, but first, I will help so-and-so with such and such.

I'll make that call to advance my career, but first, so-and-so needs me.

I just have to finish this project (that has been incomplete for almost a decade)…butt first…

It's our own butts that need saving…literally and figuratively, and we are the ones to finally decide when, where, and how. When to finally trust and when to finally reach for that safe extended hand that is offered for support and help.

There are many people who can help. We simply cannot do it on our own. We are the ones floundering out at sea, needing a life preserver, needing a rescue. A rescue from all the pain and sorrow and horrors that this world can and often does provide. I believe there are angels along the way to help guide and nurture us, some are disguised in human form. We simply must find the courage to let others help. To let them in. To let them see us at our worst with all our fears so we get a chance to be our best, despite all the pain.

Someone who can relate because they too have experienced the horrors. They understand. Someone who has been trained with a kind heart and thick skin to help direct us to and guide us through our healing process. They are able to be beacons of light and hope when we think it's impossible. Someone who can pray with us and for us in a multitude of ways, so we may find guidance and grace. Someone who can talk and help us make some sense of it all…or to just listen as we get all the demons out and clear all the cobwebs.

We get the chance to shine the light into our darkness and emerge from it strong and happy. We get to win by saying: "You may have hurt me but you DO NOT have the right to hurt or control me anymore! I get to live. I get to thrive. I get to win!" There is no need to suffer in silence anymore.

It all takes time and courage and doesn't happen overnight. But there is hope.

At first, I couldn't dare tell anyone. How would they believe me? Why would they care? Why should I dump all my woes on some innocent bystander? How could they help repair the damage that was already done. I was doomed anyway. I took the chance and started reading books, finding television shows that addressed these topics and found out that I am not alone and I do not have to suffer in silence anymore.

As it turned out, I was fortunate to have loving grandparents to raise me when my parents couldn't. It was not their fault that these things happened to me. They did the best they could.

I made peace with God when I realized that it was not his will that my mother drank and gave up, it was HER choice. She was very sad and did not know how to cope with a broken heart.

I was able to forgive both parents for abandoning me. They were both broken by their circumstances in many ways and couldn't recover.

I was able to learn that bullies are people who are desperately crying out for help. They too are often victims. I was able to find inner strength and understanding to later help bullies and their victims make better choices and live happier and healthier lives.

I was able to forgive the very sick men who molested me and the others who tried.

I made it.

I survived.

I had my power back

Now I could thrive!

I took that road less travelled and dared to reach out and accept and ask for help. Baby steps. Building trust and courage. Daring to speak my truth, no matter how painful. Embarking on a journey and having no idea where it would lead. Would I survive all this self-help stuff? Who could I talk to that could possibly help ME? Finally, with the help of some very special people in my life, I learned to heal, to forgive, and to love. There were friends to reach out to—pastors, social workers, counselors, energy workers, doctors, and groups, to name a few. There were seminars and retreats.

I am deeply grateful for all the help and support. At times, I am even proud to be survivor, especially in memory of so many who are not, for whatever reason.

All the help is there, we just need to dare and take that chance, sometimes it takes our last bit of hope, or we even have to borrow someone else's hope to see us through. We CAN make it to the other side, even if it is...butt first.

Mary E. Stevenson

Ever since she was a little girl, Mary E. Stevenson has been deeply in tune with the people and the animals around her. She has channeled this gift into vocations as a healer, animal communicator, and transformational speaker. Her first book, *Ready to Love, Fact or Fiction?* is a guide to help people find the love of their lives. It was based on her experiences with looking for love in all the wrong places before finding the one. Mary currently does healing sessions (using a variety of modalities) with people and animals to assist them in living their lives to the fullest!

www.maryestevenson.com

✉ **info@maryestevenson.com**

f **facebook.com/MaryEddyStevenson**

🐦 **twitter.com/WHHMary**

in **ca.linkedin.com/pub/mary-stevenson/26/246/88a**

Mary and I have known each other for a few years. She has a powerful story to share of a different sort, full of energy and love to everyone. Thank YOU, Mary, for being a part of this project!

~ Aime Hutton

CHAPTER 6

SENSING THE WORLD

By Mary E. Stevenson

Born a month earlier than expected, I came into the world quickly and easily early in the morning of September 11. My parents were happy to greet their second daughter into the family. Since I was a month premature, I was tiny, but I was healthy according to the doctors. My mom said I was so small that she nicknamed me Mickey Mouse. My mom said later that I seemed to be born sick because I was always having stomach issues—usually at the most inopportune times, like the day of my christening, or other big events.

I loved nature. Every moment I could be outside, I would. I loved climbing trees, playing with my dogs, collecting frogs and snakes, and playing with daddy long legs. I felt so connected to everything in nature and loved my dogs like they were my best friends.

I felt a very strong connection to God. My dad would come and pray with me every night before I'd fall asleep. I would continue my prayers, asking for blessings for all my family and friends. Throughout the day, I would ask God to change things I thought should be changed in the world and help to heal people's hearts. I couldn't understand how people treated each other at times. My heart would literally ache.

As a small child, I remember feeling so happy and then walking into a room, a family gathering, a party, or even a store, and instantly my feelings would change. I would feel stress, start to get sick to my stomach, or want to cry. These feelings would come over me like a wave and fill my body and mind. It was hard to understand why my feelings would change so quickly and be so strong! It would be like someone turned on a switch.

When I started first grade, I was thrilled to be meeting new friends. I would be happy heading off to school but then when I was there, I would have an overwhelming number of feelings running through me and often have a stomach ache. It would calm down when I would get home. On my last day of school, a friend gave me a little stuffed bear. I loved it and as I was thanking her for it, I felt this wave of jealousy coming over me. I turned around and saw another little girl, Jane, looking at me. We went outside for story time shortly after that. I was listening to the teacher read and then in my head I had a picture of Jane taking my stuffed bear. I said I had to use the washroom and I went running into my classroom and looked in my desk. The bear was gone. After story time, I told my teacher I thought Jane stole my bear. The teacher was very upset with me for accusing Jane and wouldn't look in her desk. As I was walking to my mom's car, I again felt a strong feeling come over me. I looked behind me and saw Jane. She was laughing as she shook the stuffed bear at me. I knew what I had seen in my mind was the truth. I was disappointed that the teacher hadn't believed me and had gotten upset with me instead of questioning her.

As I was going through grade school, I started to have more and more stomach aches. Quite often, I would go off by myself at recess and sit under a tree and read. I loved seeing the caterpillars and other insects. The children noticed what I was doing and they would come over, grab a caterpillar, and tear it apart in front of me and start laughing. The kids loved to do things that would make me cry. Once they noticed that I was sensitive, I was a target. One day some boys gave a girl with Down syndrome some "candies." I found out they were really ex-lax pills they'd put food coloring on but it was too late to warn her. She was happy these boys were being nice to her and giving her candy. Then she got a stomachache and ran to the washroom. I felt her hurt and was crying when my mom picked me up from school. I had so much compassion and I could not understand how people could be so cruel.

I would find myself crying, and sometimes didn't even know why. I remember thinking I didn't belong in this world. I felt so different. Why didn't other people feel the same as me? My parents weren't sure what they should do with me since I seemed to be so emotional.

If I asked to stay at home, my mom would let me. We would bake cookies, sing songs, or do crafts, and I would feel better. Of course, this would only be a short term solution.

I didn't understand why I would feel things so strongly. I also didn't understand what was happening when I could feel one way, step into a room, and instantly feel something so completely different. Because I didn't understand, I couldn't explain it to my parents. They just saw me as being a very emotional and sensitive child and didn't know how to help me. Now when people experience this, there is a label for it—empath.

Before I started sixth grade, I heard I was getting a very mean teacher. She was an older woman who was very stern and wanted things done just right. I could feel the stress from everyone in the classroom. It felt overwhelming. I did what the teacher asked of me and was doing well with my academics. However, I started to get severe headaches. I actually had no issues with my teacher. She told my parents that I was her favorite student. But as the year progressed, so did these headaches. I had one almost every day.

My health issues, the stomach aches, and headaches (migraines), brought me to the doctor's office and to the hospital throughout my childhood and beyond. No serious medical conditions were ever found.

I had a very good friend, Jenny, in junior high school who was sweet and kind. I loved being with her except when her stepfather was around. If her stepfather was near, I would get sick with a headache and have to leave. My mom noticed what was happening and decided Jenny should come to our house for visits. I kept in touch with Jenny and when she was in her late twenties, she told me that her stepfather used to sexually abuse her. At that point in time, I completely understood why I would get those headaches when I was near him.

It wasn't until my late twenties in a hypnotherapy session that I started to really understand myself. I learned quickly that I had very strong intuitive abilities and I learned how to turn them on and off. I was able to start reading people and situations as if they were a book. I could open the book and then close it when I had gotten the information I needed. I also learned I am not alone in having these abilities. There was such a relief and a healing that happened inside (physically and mentally) by being acknowledged and learning how to use these sensitivities to my advantage.

Having this strong connection to nature and animals has given me the ability to connect with animals in such a way that they actually communicate with me. The animals can show me what is going on, and often they tell me about their owners. Animals are so in tune with their owners that sometimes they take on their stress or even their physical ailments as a way of trying to help them. When I communicate with pets and this type of information comes out, I am in a position to help heal the whole family.

Having these abilities can really be a gift. They can help you to avoid situations and people that may not be good for you. When you listen, you will know clearly what is right and good for you. You can assist others in seeing things within that they may not be able to see for themselves. Once I understood and accepted them—and myself—having these strong intuitive abilities helped me tremendously in my healing work with others and in my own life.

If you have a child with these abilities, encourage them to talk about them and explain what they are experiencing. Take them to a therapist that understands these sensitivities and can teach them how to control and use them in the most effective and pleasant way. They will learn to love themselves for who they are and live a wonderful and fulfilling life!

Inch by Inch

Freyja P. Jensen

I'm an energetic, effervescent, and polished HR recruiter, networking professional, office administrator, and executive ninja with a passion for people. I'm also a mother, grandmother, daughter, and valued friend. I have a keen ability to build lasting, respected relationships and valued partnerships through media and public relations and am now looking forward to being a published and successful author! Agreeing to do this chapter meant being brave and victorious in my personal growth. I am fierce about being a champion in fighting for others by using my voice in my writing and through public speaking engagements. I wish to create hope and courage in others to realize their own authenticity, become stronger, and free themselves of their burdens to live full, happy, healthy, and loving lives.

I am here to listen and support you in your journey as a Practitioner of Life. You can connect with me on:

✉ **msfreyjapjensen@gmail.com**
f **norse.viking.goddess**
in **ca.linkedin.com/in/executiveninja**

> Freyja and I know each other through mutual friends. Her energy, spirit, and brilliance shine through her photos and her story. Thank YOU, Freyja, for being in this book project!
>
> **~ Aime Hutton**

CHAPTER 7

BABY GIRL LOST HER VOICE

By Freyja P. Jensen

It was a post on Facebook that prompted me on how to begin my chapter. It spawned some intensely painful childhood memories but added an important piece to my healing process. I was eight when Mom was killed in a horrific train crash right in front of our eyes. Mom had asked my two brothers and me to sit across from her so she could read some paperwork. That was the day we were all being reunited, as Dad had found work in the mine and gone ahead to get us a place so we could settle in. The crash happened just as we arrived at our destination. Another train derailed and came right through the side of our train car. There were three horrific bangs like thunder. I remember hearing the cracking of wood and screeching of metal and then splinters flying everywhere. My brothers and I huddled together frozen in fear. The next thing I remember is noticing the entire wall of the side of the train where my Mother sat was gone—and so was she. **I could not find my voice to scream**.

Dad was devastated and lost for a very long time. I'm not sure how many months before I felt he even realized we existed. He hired a housekeeper to take care of us. I watched her take things from the trunks that belonged to my Mother to give them to her grown daughter who would wear them around town. This made me cry. As a punishment to my older brother for wetting the bed—a result of the trauma he experienced—she would wrap the sheets around his head and beat him with a broom. When she left me in the care of her oldest son, he molested me. I told her this and she beat me and washed out my mouth with soap. She said if I told anyone she would make sure I would not forget. I could not go to my father, nor did I know of anyone else to go to that I felt safe with. It must have been my fault. **My voice did not count.**

My mother had always washed, brushed, and braided my long, beautiful golden locks every day. Those were precious moments that belonged to only Mom and me. My hair adorned me and made me feel like a beautiful princess. I was sent to a hairdresser's home who had been told to cut off my hair, right above the elastic at the pony tail. I cried and felt crushed. I was sent home with the pony tail in my hand. I felt ugly. I felt alone. I felt lost. **My voice cracked.**

I was bullied in school. Told I was ugly and that the clothes (that my mother had sewn for me) must have come from the dump. I was threatened by a girl in school who made me so afraid I just wanted to hide. I was petrified. **My voice was subdued**.

Dad remarried. As I matured, I was compared to my mom by my stepmom. "You have ugly lips and legs like your Mom and you will be just like her." (I can't say what she called her here). I felt her words were emotionally retarding me. *I wanted to scream for someone to hear me, see me, love me. I felt invisible and alone. My words meant nothing.* **My voice was squashed.**

When I was having trouble at school, I was constantly told I must be stupid for "not getting it" and that I would never amount to anything—that I would be a failure. **I could feel my words choking me in my throat but I could not get them out.** I was punished in many horrific ways that I won't speak of here today. They were degrading and humiliating, and as a young girl maturing into a young woman, they were hugely detrimental to my emotional and sexual being.

The harshest moments came when my siblings and I were left in the care of someone we were told could be trusted. I was confined, tied up, gagged, and blind-folded. I was a victim of rape for the first time at twelve. I was mentally controlled to believe I deserved it and would always be indebted to that person because he did me a favor. He came back for more when I was twenty-eight. It was then that I finally said **enough**. At that moment, **I reclaimed my voice**.

THE LESSON AND THE MESSAGE

The little girl inside me cries still sometimes because of her fears and difficulty trusting. The woman in me raises her voice and is aware that her beauty is charming but that it is the light from within that shines brightest. The woman claims her power and protects that little girl. That little girl needs to rest and be reassured that everything is going to be just fine. The woman, ME, has recovered—a survivor! Every day I work at manifesting the wonderful, powerful, glorious, strong, wise, independent, and healthy lady I am. Each day I live with passion for life, love, and people, authentically and with purpose. **I am an advocate for those that have lost their voice**. I was named after a Norse Viking warrior goddess by my mother, and I claim that power every day and so can you. We must learn to listen to our inner voice, trust our heart, and *hear* and *do*. Take action. Walk the walk. Surround ourselves with others on the same path that are learning and growing from our experiences. See them as life lessons. Forgive. Teach our children that it is OK to speak up and not be afraid to use their voices and be heard. One of my greatest lessons was from my son, who is now a grown man I am proud of, with an amazing child of his own. He came to me via his school guidance counselor many years ago and asked me to just listen because what he had to say was important. I did. It was a powerful learning experience. I am still learning to listen better. I am far from perfect, I am perfectly imperfect and that is perfectly OK. I am accepting that and learning to just be OK with me as I am. I am amazing and so are you.

I have also lost both of my brothers tragically, and stepmother, but Dad remains and he is also stronger. Forgiveness heals. He is better. I am better. I have my son, his beautiful partner, and my amazing granddaughter. I've failed at many things but always pick myself back up again. I am blessed with many friends who love and believe in me. **Thank you all for seeing me, loving me, and hearing my voice. I am grateful for the lessons.**

"Listening is a magnetic and strange thing, a creative force. The friends who listen to us are the ones we move toward. When we are listened to, it creates us, makes us unfold, and expand."

~ Karl A. Menniger

I am here to listen and support you in your journey as a Practitioner of Life. You can connect with me on Facebook as norse.viking. goddess or by email at msfreyjapjensen@gmail.com or on LinkedIn as ca.linkedin.com/in/executiveninja/

Susan Rear

Susan is a daughter, wife, mother, and grandmother. Her greatest joys are her two wonderful granddaughters: Sydney and Justice. She lives with her husband of forty-five years in the town of High River, Alberta, Canada. She is a dreamer, a writer of poetry, and the holder of the songs of her family. Her belief in the beauty and support of angels brings peace and harmony to all that she experiences in life. Susan works in the health care system in a variety of positions, sharing her compassion and understanding for anyone requiring a kind word and gentle hug.

Susan is Loree's mum and Sydney's grandmother! She is amazing and has transformed through this process! Thank YOU, Susan, for your spirit and energy for this book project!

~ Aime Hutton

CHAPTER 8

JUST BREATHE

By Susan Rear

The day my granddaughter was born, I watched my daughter experience the joy of having a daughter of her own and the overwhelming fear of losing her as she was rushed to the NICU. I saw them both for only moments. My granddaughter was beautiful. She wrapped her tiny hand around my little finger and stole my heart. My daughter was exhausted, frightened; I only had time to give her an encouraging hug before I was ushered from the room. Hours later the families were told our precious little granddaughter had been born with Down syndrome. She was having breathing difficulties, and they suspected heart complications. The fear of losing my granddaughter mingled with my fear for my daughter. She looked so pale, so drawn. Where would she find the stamina, the courage to face the days ahead? How would she ever survive if her baby girl didn't?

I totally underestimated my daughter. Over the next week, I watched her deal with doctors, nurses, monitoring machines, alarms, breast pumps, and the fact she could only hold her baby for short periods of time. She displayed a strength that amazed me. Existing on cat naps, she cuddled, coaxed, and literally willed her daughter to live. "Just breathe" became her motto—just take that next step! She fought hard just as her little daughter fought hard and together they celebrated a victory. My daughter was allowed to bring her baby home. We didn't realize it at the time, but in a few short years, the remarkable bond they formed in those first few days would be tested again. This time the battle would be much longer, the cost both physically and emotionally enormous. But their great love for each other would once again play the most important role in the final outcome.

The next few years seemed to fly by. My granddaughter was a happy, content baby, just as her mother had been. She seldom cried and when things weren't OK in her world, I would gather her close and rock her in our favorite chair while singing the songs of my childhood. It was our special time.

My daughter never stopped searching for ways to stimulate the low muscle tone and poor appetite that is consistent for children born with Down syndrome. The downstairs area in their home soon became full of play stations—sand boxes, water tables, slides, and tunnels provided fun-filled hours of exercise. A storybook nook, an artist's corner supplied cuddle time, and creative play involving those tiny fingers and eyes, which were covered with the smallest pair of glasses I'd ever seen. I was in awe of the inventiveness my daughter displayed. My granddaughter faced many challenges, such as walking and talking, but she found her own way to accomplish things. It may have taken a little longer and required a lot more effort, but she persisted and her mommy was her biggest cheerleader.

In the early months of 2001, my granddaughter's health began to decline; unbeknownst to us, an enemy was invading her body. The many doctors' appointments brought no conclusive results, but my daughter knew there was something terribly wrong and persisted. In December 2001, my three-year-old granddaughter was diagnosed with a rare form of leukemia. The cancer was aggressive, thus the treatment also had to be aggressive. There was such a fine line between what type of chemotherapy would halt the disease— saving the child—and what type of chemotherapy would kill her. "Just breathe" once again became the way to control the fear as we struggled through those first terrifying weeks.

Once again, I watched as my daughter and son-in-law took on the medical profession to find the very best treatment protocol for their daughter. They spent hours on the computer researching and compiling data showing the pros and cons of different treatments. They called upon friends and relatives involved in the world of cancer for advice on how to proceed, as they'd only have one chance to defeat this new threat to their daughter's life. Just days before Christmas 2001, the fight to save my granddaughter's life began—a journey that would start with that first step and continue one step at a time.

My daughter wanted to ensure the hospital stay was as normal as possible for a three year old, so she created fantasy rooms filled with love, laughter, music, and people dressed as favorite Disney characters. This wasn't always workable, as she also had to accommodate the many machines, drugs, doctors, nurses, and medical interruptions that were keeping my granddaughter alive. The next months were indescribable—some procedures terrifying, some heartbreaking, many experimental. Through the process, my granddaughter was never alone; one or all of us were always with her.

During one difficult fifty-two-day period, other than to shower, my daughter never left her daughter's side because even the medical staff feared she would be unable to survive the war raging in her little body. One night, while curled upon a cot watching my daughter comfort my granddaughter as she suffered unbearable pain I heard her say, "It's okay Darling, if you're too tired to go on Mommy will be fine, if you want to go with the Angels my Darling it's okay." Silent tears rolled down my face as I marveled at the love in her voice, what courage, rather than have her continue in agony she unselfishly was willing to let the Angels take her home. I have always felt that was the night my granddaughter began to recover.

The whole oncology unit cheered and cried when, finally, my tiny granddaughter, tightly clutching her IV pole, took her first faltering steps out of that dreaded isolation room. A miracle, maybe—but if so, in my heart I know it was the love of a mother for her daughter and the love of a daughter for her mommy that made that miracle possible.

I only really held my daughter twice through this whole nightmare called cancer—that was the total number of times she allowed herself the luxury of surrendering to her fears. The sobs were heart-wrenching as she dealt with the horror of what her daughter was experiencing, but they were also short lived; her daughter was waiting. Months later, when we finally came home, my granddaughter was a shadow of her former self. She had no immune system and couldn't have a lot of visitors. She also had no appetite and wouldn't eat, and she wasn't all that comfortable at home because she hadn't actually lived there for over eight months. My daughter once again came up with ingenious ways to help her daughter cope with all these new and scary situations. Little by little, my daughter rebuilt her daughter's trust in her surroundings, her confidence in her ability to accomplish small tasks, and her health. In doing so, she gave her back the joy of just being a child. Their astonishing bond, forged in those first few days of my granddaughter's life, remained unbroken. Together their family had fought cancer and together they had survived.

My daughter now faced her own health issues. She managed these with the same courage and determination she had displayed over the years. She just kept breathing. She never once faltered in her efforts to make sure her daughter continued to thrive. These years were filled with many challenges, which were met with a willingness to change in order to ensure the best possible outcome for everyone. It became a learning time for my daughter and granddaughter—each day, each experience they shared, brought them such excitement and happiness. Their lives became a great adventure.

Today, sixteen years later, my daughter and granddaughter continue their amazing journey together. They address many issues facing special needs children—they give presentations to various groups including schools, service clubs, and most importantly, my granddaughter's peers. My daughter has always made sure my granddaughter was able to attend schools with an "inclusion program." My daughter's tireless involvement in this process has allowed my granddaughter to form lasting friendships with her classmates. It brings hope and a sense of peace to my life to see her enjoying typical teenage outings with her girlfriends. My granddaughter has limited speech but has no problem communicating her thoughts and feelings to those around her. Her mother, although often a little apprehensive, encourages her daughter to experience life on her own terms, to try new things, and to "just breathe."

I find myself marveling at the loving connection that has, over the years, developed between these two special people. I am forever grateful that I have been able to support their journey and help with the many challenges these two have encountered. My wish, as their journey continues, is to be available when needed, to comfort when possible, and to always applaud their astonishing accomplishments. I know they realize they are cradled lovingly within my heart.

Loree Cowling

Loree is a speaker, storyteller, coach, intuitive healer, and writer who helps people connect to their hearts. She combines the techniques, skills, and wisdom acquired over the past fourteen years as an intuitive healer and coach—along with her experience raising a daughter who has chosen to shine her light as a beautiful soul with Down syndrome—to reveal the sacred gifts within all of us that allow one to live an authentic life. Whether speaking at events with her daughter, telling stories, or doing one-on-one sessions, Loree helps people connect to their own inner wisdom and truth.

www.loreecowling.com

✉ **loree@loreecowling.com**

f **facebook.com/pages/Loree-Cowling-Connection-to-Heart/476762675671168**

f **facebook.com/loree.cowling**

I have known Loree for a few years now. To have her incredible story about her daughter in this book was a must! She's amazing and I knew she just had to be in the book! Thank YOU, Loree!

~ Aime Hutton

CHAPTER 9

CONNECTION TO HEART

By Loree Cowling

When I was expecting my daughter, people would tell me how it would change my life and I would become more than I ever thought possible. I could never have imagined the depth my heart would be affected by the gift of becoming a mom. The excitement while I carried her was tempered by the underlying doubt towards my ability to be wholly and completely responsible for another human being. Yet I still believed that the moment she was born, I would feel the rush of love that was so eloquently described to me.

I don't remember that. I remember a stillness. As if even taking a breath would somehow shatter the careful illusion that I had created within myself—that I was more than ready, capable, and prepared to be a mother. The stillness was not born from the peace of deep inner wisdom and connection. The stillness was created from fear.

Fear that my four-week-premature baby girl was not OK. Fear that if she was alright, I wouldn't be able to care for her properly. When I held her for the first time, I could barely breathe and waited to hear someone tell me everything would be alright. That she was perfect and healthy. I was waiting to hear the words, "You will do just fine. You can learn the joys of life together. You will grow into the mother you were meant to be." Instead, I heard a doctor telling me they believed she had Down syndrome, and she wasn't getting enough oxygen so would be moved into the special care unit until they figured out the cause. I felt my heart stop.

The next time I saw my beautiful girl, they were doing an ultrasound on her heart and I found myself taken back to a TV show from the 1970s I had seen a few weeks earlier. It depicted a baby girl born with Down syndrome and a heart condition and they'd just given up on her. They let that baby die because they felt it would be a less cruel life than if she lived. This was the only reference I had about having a child with Down syndrome. I thought that if they found a problem, they would let her die. They found four heart abnormalities and I fought panic as terror gripped me in a way I truly cannot describe. It did not matter to me if she was "different" than I expected, she was beautiful and perfect to me. I sat in a wheelchair, completely exhausted, watching my tiny baby surrounded by machines, but inside I was screaming: "Don't let my baby die! I won't let you! You can't have her!" This was only the first of several times in her life I would be screaming these words in my heart and mind.

All of the dreams I thought I had about the way my family would look shattered that day. In that moment, the internal focus for everything I did became about keeping Sydney alive and safe. I forgot to breathe! It seemed as if I would never get enough oxygen again. That's the thing about fear, it robs you of vital life breath.

We took Sydney home seven days later, and I went about creating what seemed like a typical life. The fear, though still there, became quiet and life was filled with so many beautiful moments as my baby became a little girl. I did the best I could, learning to be a mom and giving her the things that would make her life full and enjoyable. Her laughter and love for life touched everyone. She would hold my face between her little hands and look lovingly into my eyes. I always believed she was willing me to hear her thoughts and dreams.

As typical childhood milestones came and went, I tried to ignore the concerns that teased my thoughts. I got stuck on her learning to walk, secretly harboring a constant concern it might never happen. Sydney had her own plans on how this life development would go and found plenty of ways to get around without the need of taking steps. It is no surprise to me that the lessons of patience, acceptance, and celebration I learned watching Sydney work on this milestone would become important later in her life. She began to walk at twenty-two months.

At two and a half, she became sick with a virus and never seemed to recover. At the age of three, Sydney was diagnosed with a rare form of leukemia and I found myself once again paralyzed by the fear that had hidden just under the surface of my being for her entire life. The day we drove Sydney to the hospital to begin treatment, I was overwhelmed by the most terrifying feeling that I was taking her to her death. Years later, I still cannot focus on this memory for more than a few minutes without feeling the intense pain of that day in my heart. For eight months, my amazingly brave daughter endured things that, in every sense, was the same as being tortured. She did this with her customary "live in the moment" attitude that allowed her to experience everything with the wonderment of a child. When not doing well physically, she gave completely into the experience and her body shut down several times sending her to the ICU. When she was feeling well, she lived with such joy that she effectively brightened the lives of all of us. Late at night, after the doctors left, we would sneak out to the nurses' station and have "movie nights" complete with laughter and popcorn and Sydney wearing her favorite rain coat and slippers.

Back then, I did not have the same amazing ability as Sydney to live in the moment, and any joy I was showing to the outside world certainly did not match the constant fear and heartache I was feeling on the inside. Her physical recovery took several years after the actual treatment was done. By the time she started to regain her health, I had become so depleted that a serious health crisis showed up in my own life. I allowed myself to become so physically, emotionally, and mentally checked out from the world around me that I lived on some odd sort of autopilot. When I decided to focus on my health and put my heart back together, I began to breathe again.

At one of our hospital follow-up visits, a nurse shared with me how her family carried a significant risk of a genetic anomaly that could affect her children if she chose to give birth. She had decided against having children—until spending time with Sydney changed her mind. She'd had testing done and was now expecting. Throughout Sydney's life, I have heard dozens of stories of how she affected people's outlooks and perceptions of the world. Sydney touches people's hearts simply by loving them exactly as they are in any given moment. Her ability to find the joy in every situation inspired me to begin to see my own life filled with miracles and gratitude.

I started doing presentations in Sydney's classroom to give her peers the opportunity to know her and spend time in her world. It quickly became clear that when people are given a chance to step into a new perception, they see others and themselves in a more understanding way. Sydney's speech is not always clear, and yet, when we stand in front of an audience, the loving nature of her being shines so brightly everyone seems to know exactly the message we are sharing. This year we spoke to over eight hundred teachers and administrators who were deeply affected by the clarity in her words and message as Sydney sang along to the song, "Perfect." After singing, she said, "I see you perfect exactly as you are." Acceptance can seem difficult when faced with the challenges of life. We struggle to accept those around us. We struggle to accept ourselves. Sydney has taught me that everyone is unique and deserves love without conditions.

In a presentation we did at her school, a student asked why it took Sydney so long to go down the stairs. I explained that in treatment, she spent fifty-two days in bed and had to learn how to walk again. It requires concentration, focus, and constant determination. Kids began giving her encouraging words, high fives, or simply stopping to wait for her. Daily, I am amazed at how her incredible spirit can affect the actions of dozens of people.

Sydney is sixteen now and wakes up every day saying, "Hello day! Let's get started." I am forever grateful that I have seen my daughter learn to walk...twice—in her own time, in her own way—always shining the brightest light for us to see the beauty in our own uniqueness.

Inch by Inch

Wendy Stefanko

My name is Wendy Stefanko. I grew up in a small town in Pennsylvania at the foot of the Allegheny mountains. I am married to my high school sweetheart and we have three sons who have grown into three wonderful men. I am a graduate of the University of Pennsylvania at Johnstown with an associate's degree in health sciences and am certified in polysomnography (sleep disorders) from California College of Health Sciences. I worked many years as a registered respiratory therapist and specialized in sleep medicine. I have won several literary awards and I am published by the PSRC.

✉ **wendy.stefanko@gmail.com**

Wendy is friends with a fellow author in this book. Her story is powerful. Wendy signed on to do this book early and has been a champion for me ever since! Thank YOU, Wendy!

~ **Aime Hutton**

CHAPTER 10

INNOCENCE LOST

By Wendy Stefanko

We post our nostalgic pictures on Facebook, depicting "the good old days" and reminisce at family gatherings and reunions, telling our stories to our children and grandchildren. We tell them it was a kinder, simpler time and we usually begin with "When I was a kid…"

We had no concept of 9/11, Columbine, or Sandy Hook. We walked without thought or care to our friend's houses after school and played outside until dark, usually arriving home ten minutes late—sweaty, exhausted, and ready to do it all over again tomorrow.

Sadly, it is a time of innocence lost. Our children are growing up in the shadows of mass violence and school shootings. As parents and a society, we are taking every step we can to prevent further tragedies, but we will never again know what it is like not to be searched at airports or have to go through metal detectors to pick our kids up at school.

But there is still another danger out there, often overlooked, as the headlines focus on the heinous tragedies mentioned above. We cannot forget about the oldest and least suspected danger to our children—the pedophile. Pedophiles are like chameleons. They often hide in plain sight under the guise of family and friends and manifest as trusted adults, such as a coach or babysitter. Tragically, they too often turn out to be family members. Pedophiles are usually well-liked and go out of their way to gain the trust of both children and adults. They get to know their victims, and in fact, they handpick them, making the child feel special by a process called "grooming" in order to gain the child—and even the parents'—trust. After a child has been abused, the pedophile uses fear and shame to threaten the child or their family if the child tells of the abuse.

Abuse can be habitual and often continues for years, but even one single event can damage a child for life, setting off a cycle of self-inflicted judgment and pain. Most victims never tell, or wait until well into their adulthood to speak up. Usually by the time a victim of childhood sexual abuse tells anyone, they are adults seeking treatment for anxiety and depression—common symptoms of post-traumatic stress disorder, which can appear years or even decades after the abuse occurred.

I was nine when I was assaulted. I was feeling very grown up, finally being allowed to walk to the library or stay for afterschool activities without having to have my older sister walk me home. We lived in a small town where everyone knew each other by name, and there was always plenty of neighborhood kids around for a pick-up game of kickball or four square.

There was no organized animal control in our town, and so Helen Thompson, the local beautician, ran an unofficial dog rescue. If anyone lost or found a pet, she was who you would call. Helen had kennels in her garage for the rare unclaimed dogs and paid fifth and sixth grade girls to walk them after school and in the summer. To be picked to be a dog walker was a job coveted by most of the girls in town, and I was one of them.

I could be shy around strangers and I liked to read, but I loved animals. I was always rescuing a baby bird or rabbit, and my dream was to be a veterinarian. We had a cat and dog that had always been willing participants as my playmates. I just loved animals, and when I was old enough I wanted to walk the dogs.

It took all the courage I could muster to go into the beauty shop and ask if I could be a dog walker. I was told I had to go talk to Charles—that he was in charge of who walked the dogs. Charles was known around town as "Simple Charles." He lived in the local boarding house for men on Main Street. Everyone in town knew Charles. He was a little odd but he always said hello when you walked by.

I again mustered my courage and asked Charles if I could walk the dogs. He told me to come inside, and I remember feeling uneasy as I followed him upstairs and into his room. It was an old house and it didn't smell very nice. He told me to have a seat on the chair next to his bed and he sat on the bed beside me.

He asked me some questions, and then after several minutes, he touched me on my upper arm, rubbing it. I remember feeling uncomfortable, but I was told to be polite and always respect my elders. When he asked me if I liked it, I did not know what to say. I was afraid he would think I was rude, so I said it was OK. He told me to come back the next day and he would decide if I could walk the dogs.

I returned the next day and Charles again told me to follow him up the stairs to his room. I again sat on the chair beside his bed. I was feeling uneasy again as he sat on the bed next to me. It was hot in his room and the muskiness of the air was heavy and unpleasant. This time, instead of touching my arm he rubbed my calf, again asking me if I liked it. I felt increasingly uncomfortable. My understanding of sex was very limited and consisted of half-truths and innuendos. Despite my uneasiness, I did not comprehend the danger I was in.

I believe at that point, my motivation shifted from my wanting to walk the dogs to obedience from my strict upbringing. I was taught that I must always be polite and respect my elders. I again told him it was OK. He took me back outside and told me I could walk the dogs and to be at the garage behind the beauty shop the next morning.

I was relieved to be out of the boarding house and in the fresh air. I let the excitement of being chosen to walk the dogs enfold me, and at supper I told my family. Dad seemed proud, and I never mentioned that Charles had taken me to his room or that he touched me. Dad told me I had to take the job seriously and that I could not miss work or let the dogs get loose. I felt like I had to make him proud.

The next morning, I went to the garage where the kennels were. Charles showed me how to handle the dogs and where I was to take them. I remember walking the dogs several times and enjoying the sunny spring days. On Saturday, Mom and Dad left for the day to go shopping and allowed me to stay home so I could walk the dogs.

I walked the dogs just like I had for several days. I left early while it was still cool, but it was getting warm by the time I brought them back to their kennels. I put them in their kennels and made sure they had enough food and water. It was rather dim in the garage and the light was streaming through one window, making the green dullness of the room a little brighter as particles of dust and dog hair danced in the ray of light.

The next thing I knew, I was being pushed down into the corner. I remember a sense of Charles being over top of me. I could smell a combination of freshly laundered clothing and his sweaty masculinity as I finally pushed him off of me and I ran out into the fresh air and sunlight of the alley. I spit and wiped my mouth out with my shirt.

I don't remember walking or running home. My sister was not back yet and had the house key, so I hid in the backyard until she came home. I slept on the floor that night, afraid that if I got into bed, my sister would somehow know what had taken place.

Tragically, I was too afraid to tell anyone what happened and I went back the next day. The girl in the beauty shop told me they no longer needed me to walk the dogs. At the time, I could not fully comprehend what had happened. I was so overwhelmed by shame and guilt, I couldn't bring myself to tell. I never told anyone until I was well into my forties. Eventually, I was able to talk about what had happened and begin to allow myself heal. My hope is that by telling my story, other parents will become aware of the often hidden signs of childhood sexual abuse, the danger of pedophiles, and the extent they will go to get to their victims.

Inch by Inch

Angel Tucker-Carr

Angel Tucker-Carr, CPLC, owner of Salon Sweet, barber, speaker, mentor, and author of multiple books, including *Little Betsy Mae*. She is the founder of Dare to Bare Your Beauty and owner of Dream In Style Event Hall. Angel is married to an amazing man and has three beautiful children.

www.angeltucker-carr.com

Angel and I met through a mutual friend on Google Plus. Her story is touching and amazing. Thank YOU, Angel, for being in this book project with us!

~ **Aime Hutton**

CHAPTER 11

FAITH REFINED

By Angel Tucker-Carr

I sat on the side of that less-than-comfortable, slightly-cushioned slab which resembled a bed, draped with a paper runner, inside of a 7 x 7 room, my legs nervously alternating kicks. I was a long ways from anxious so it was clearly the nerves powering my swinging legs. I could hear paper sheets being ripped off of cushioned slabs as a mixture of voices simultaneously traveled to my ears—syllable by syllable. Through the thin walls that separated me from the next patient, I heard the tone of my doctor's voice closing the meeting with the patient before me.

"Well, good morning, Angel! How are you today?" My response was always one of two—*I don't know yet*, or *I'm doing alright*. After we had our normal conversation about our kids and how they are growing up, and talking about our spouses and what they are doing these days, we got to the reason I was there. I'd been a patient of my doctor's since 1996, when I reluctantly had to change doctors due to my insurance company's network. It wasn't long before I realized that the change was not a bad one at all. Although I respected and trusted my previous gynecologist, I knew that God was looking out for me when my previous GYN referred me to my current GYN. I had a history of female problems since I was in my early high school years, so I kept routine checks. I didn't know if it was hereditary because my mom also had problems early on, or if I had them because of an early sexual violation I encountered as a girl, shortly before the problems began. To this date…I still don't know.

When I was treated for precancerous cells on my cervix in 1993, my then doctor told me if I wanted to have children I'd better start immediately. Well, I already had one child and another one was not in the plan. One child was enough. Although we were proud parents, time and money didn't allow us to think past the bank account to have another baby. I was a firm believer that *what was meant to be was going to be.*

About four years later, I became pregnant with my middle child, Gabriel. Michael was about seven years old at the time.

In October of 1999, I began to have some problems inside of my abdomen and pelvic area that were too much for me to ignore. My activities continued but it became a bit complicated to perform at the level I was use to competing at. I finally went to the doctor and found out that I had a dermoid tumor in my abdominal wall. It was small but needed to be addressed. I was in constant pain. I was in a continuous battle to feel and look good at that point. I had already had one unsuccessful procedure to remove the tumor, but only scar tissue was removed. A couple of months later, still carrying that tumor, I became even sicker. What I thought was a urinary tract infection turned out to be the news that I didn't want to hear at all. Sitting there, looking my doctor right in the eyes, these words flowed from his lips.

"Angel, you're pregnant!" I was by no means happy. I mean, after all, the last time I was sitting before him he had concerns of having the tumor removed. Now we had a pregnancy to deal with. I'd already been told that I would need to have the tumor removed by a general surgeon, and anyone who knows me, knows that I don't like "change." It was the beginning of nine months of hell.

During one of my visits to the surgeon, we had an interesting conversation. I still remember these words that he spoke to me, fourteen years later. "You have two children and a husband to live for. Why are you trying to have this baby?" At first, I didn't think anything of his words. Remember, I didn't want to have another child and it did seem stupid that I got pregnant in the midst of health problems. He advised me to abort this child because of the complications I was experiencing, and the prognosis didn't look good. The tumor was growing as quickly as the baby. I was told that either I would die, the baby would die, or both of us would die. I didn't like any of those deals! He said, "I hope you have your timing right and know exactly how far along you are because as soon as you turn sixteen weeks, you need to go to the hospital and check in. The tumor must be removed if you're going to go through with the pregnancy!" I really didn't want to have a baby, but I knew that she was my baby! My husband and I didn't necessarily want a child at this time, but we wanted our child! I had another routine visit with my GYN before the sixteen weeks and I told him what the doctor said. I didn't need an interpreter to tell me what he was thinking. He immediately made one statement, "Angel, where is your faith?"

And then, I was sixteen weeks...

I couldn't be given any anesthesia because of my pregnancy, so everything had to go on inside of the operating room. The operating room was so full that I didn't know how they would all fit. Every head and their team was there—NICU, my OB/GYN, the anesthesiologist, and of course, the surgical team was there. I was guided through what I was about to experience, and it was by far the scariest thing I've ever experienced. The voice said, "You will see different shades of gray and then a shade of black, but don't be afraid." That's the last thing I remember before waking up.

I was bandaged from beneath my breast down past my cesarean scar and taped all around, with twenty-seven staples to top it off. The pain was paralyzing. I was four months pregnant, stapled diagonally across my stomach, and had two drain tubes that constantly filled up with fluid stitched inside of my stomach to go home with. Three quarters of my abdominal muscles were cut out—my body would never look the same.

Six more months of misery, but I worked a normal shift. I had doctor appointment after appointment. Toward the end of my pregnancy, around seven months, I started seeing three doctors a week. One appointment per week was to check my fluid level.

November 8, 2000, I went to my appointment on my way to work and my doctor told me to go to the hospital immediately because I was in labor. I went to the hospital after calling in sick (I know it sounds funny but it's true). I was doing Word Finds while waiting. I was being kept by something greater than myself. I had faith that I had been kept and all was going to be alright.

My daughter was delivered shortly after 1:30 p.m. and she was perfectly normal, healthy, and beautiful. Her name is Taylor Michelle Carr. She has been a blessing to our family. I often think about the "what ifs" and what would my life be like without her had I not heard the words, "Where is your faith?"

Through all of the tears, fears, ups and downs, and even the joys, my life has never been the same. I have the physical scars to remind me of so many things: the power of believing, the power of words, and my faith. I would do it all over if given the same results. My finances weren't ready for another child, and I sure didn't want to leave my boys (the loves of my life) and my amazing husband to have another child; but she wasn't just any child…she was *my* child!

We don't have the answers to everything or why we have to go through some things, but the main thing is *knowing* that we are not alone. What I went through made me tougher, stronger, and the amazing woman that I am. For every life on earth, there is a purpose.

Taylor is a scholar athlete and Christian girl who is truly amazing. She plays volleyball, basketball, golf, softball, runs track, does gymnastics, and plays in the band. She graduated from Barbizon Acting and Modeling School, was a state finalist for National American Miss, and has received many academic awards. This year she received the highest award given at her middle school—the Bill Coplin Award. Her name will be on a plaque in the hallway for all to see throughout the life of that school.

The decision I made is all because someone who cared reminded to look to my faith at the right time.

Inch by Inch

Jeffrey L. May

Jeff L. May is the chief executive officer of *ApexSCF*

Jeff draws upon his in-depth experience with over twenty-five years in law enforcement, fire, and EMS.

Jeff served as, chief of police, police officer, deputy sheriff, director of the Adam Walsh Sexual Assault Notification Program, law enforcement training officer, domestic violence coordinator, terrorism liaison officer, firemen, medic, and fire captain.

Jeff was very successful within the law enforcement and fire department profession.

www.apexscf.com

✉ **apexscf@gmail.com**

f **facebook.com/ApexSCF**

Jeffrey and I met through the networking of eWomen Network. His passion to help others is amazing and I respect and honor him for this. Thank YOU, Jeffrey, for being in this book project!

~ **Aime Hutton**

CHAPTER 12

BAD THINGS HAPPEN TO GOOD PEOPLE
By Jeffrey L. May

Bad things happen to good people; this is an unfortunate fact in our society. Any one of us can be a victim of a crime that threatens our personal safety or the safety of our families. We cannot control the actions of others, but we don't have to remain powerless either. We can choose to step out of the victim loop and take personal responsibility and accountability for our safety.

As a little boy of about five years old, I witnessed an extremely violent crime toward my mother and father that could have taken their lives. A neighbor man—we will call him "Jim"—lived right next door to us for three years. All that time we lived in fear of this person. We had seen police cars many times at Jim's house over the years but Jim always remained.

This one afternoon seemed just like any other but this was going to be a day like no other, and one we will never forget.

Mom noticed Jim and his wife on their horses and they had my fifteen-year-old sister and her horse pinned against the fence. Mom yelled at them to leave her daughter alone and immediately ran over to help my sister. When Jim saw my mom heading toward them, he got off the horse and walked over to his truck. Jim pulled out a large axe handle that was behind the seat and hid it behind his leg. My sister was screaming for help and my mom was frantically trying to get her to safety. Right about this time, my dad, who was just getting home, pulled into the driveway and saw the commotion. Dad heard my mom and sister screaming and ran over to help. Dad stepped in front of Jim to shield my mom and he was hit in the head with the axe handle. This crazy person swung that ax handle so hard that it knocked him to the ground and rendered him unconscious. I remember mom screaming for us, my brother and sisters, to get into the house. "Run!" She screamed like I had never heard before. We did—we ran as fast as we could back into the house.

Many of the neighbors heard my mom screaming for help. They ran to my mother and father's aid while Jim was sitting on top of my dad, violently punching him in the head over and over. Mom was able to grab a hammer out of my dad's truck, and while this crazy man was trying to kill my father, my mother used the only thing she could to save my dad's life. With the hammer, she struck Jim in the head, knocking him off my dad, saving his life. My dad was able to fight back and was now on top of Jim, fighting for his life and protecting our family. One of the neighbors ran over with a handgun that he was going to use to save my dad's life with. Remember, all of the other neighbors were very afraid and intimated by Jim, but at that moment, many of our neighbors put aside their fears and came to the aid my family. My dad was focused on fighting back and protecting his family from this crazy person. The neighbors had to pull Dad off Jim now that they had a weapon to get control of the situation.

I remember it vividly like it was yesterday. This extremely violent attack was happening as I was standing in the living room, looking out the big window. I was frozen in fear, crying so much that it was hard to catch my breath. My sisters were running around screaming and crying for anyone to come and help us. We all thought our mom and dad were going to be killed that day right in front of us. As little children, we couldn't do anything about it, just stand there horrified, watching in disbelief. I was just a little boy but the little man inside of me really wanted to do so much more. I was scared to death and felt helpless. I wished I was bigger to help my parents but I wasn't. It was the worst feeling. Now looking back on that day, God help the crazy person that would ever try hurt anyone in my family now.

Jim went to the hospital and then off to jail that day. My dad had also went to the hospital—he had to have over three hundred stitches in his head and face.

We all recovered from that very horrific day and moved on to live very good lives. Jim went to jail for a long time. (Good!). We'd lived next to this crazy person for three years, never imagining we could be victims. Once Jim was released from jail, he and his wife were forced out of our neighborhood. In the days leading up to their departure from our block, we never heard a word out of his mouth—no more problems and no interaction at all. Maybe it was because my father took a stand that day and fought back in the face of danger when the odds were stacked against him.

From that day on, there has always been something in me to help others. I went into the boy scouts, and as I got older, into the martial arts for many years. Then I started my career in fire and medical. I knew that it was my job to protect not only my family but anyone that needed my help. I spent many years doing just that, but I felt that I could do more from the law enforcement side so I put myself through the police academy. I did this while keeping my fulltime job as a fire captain with the state of Nevada. I went into the law enforcement field, working my way up to the rank of chief of police. Even with all I have done to help others, I still felt there was something missing. I was tired of always coming in *after*…after the damage was done, the crime committed, the victims hurt. Was there more I could do to equip others so the everyday person could protect themselves? Yes! I dived into building my own program, taking all of my knowledge and experience to help people *before* they became victims. This was one of the most difficult undertakings but by far it has been one of the most rewarding things I have ever done in my life.

It is my true dream and desire to help others and giving back is what we do best at *ApexSCF*. There needs to come a time when we can be safe—safe to walk the streets any time of day or night, safe to sleep with our doors unlocked, safe to sleep with our windows open, safe to let our children play down the street and have fun, safe for our children to go to school and learn, and safe to live without fear.

Looking back at that day when I was five years old, it was one of the worst things a child should ever have to witness. I truly believe that day was one of the building blocks in my life. I never wanted to feel that helpless pain again. Whether it is my own family or a stranger on the street that can't stand up and fight or protect themselves, I can and will help. We all need to be strong for the people that can't, the ones that need us, that helping hand, that voice that says *I am here to help*. We all have it in us to get back up and keep on fighting—to never give up. I'm not saying that it's easy. It may be the hardest thing you will ever go through in life but you can get through anything—you just have to be there to do it. So *be there and do it*. Trust me when I say, I know what real pain feels like and I will tell you there are some days that I need help from my loved ones and God, but I still get up every morning and face a new day with hope and a heartfelt commitment to always give my best in that day.

My dad told me once, "Son, when God brings the tough things in our lives, it's his way of getting us ready for the real hard things to come, so we will have the strength to handle it."

My story is dedicated to my mom and dad—when the chips were down, they never quit. I wish I could have been older on that day so I could have been there to help my dad from getting hurt. I love you guys, and thank you for always being there for me.

Inch by **Inch**

Michelle E. Wood

Michelle has two beautiful children and she strives every day to make them into strong individuals, giving them the freedom to flourish and grow in their very own unique ways. Michelle teaches them at home the skills she thinks they will require to succeed in life, giving them every opportunity she can. She also runs her own business: Purity — School of Spirituality. Her business is within the healing industry and she herself found that her ways worked to get her onto her road of recovery. She does her utmost to provide this for her clients and students, surrounding them with loving support always.

Michelle welcomes you into her light by contacting her through any of the links available:

www.meharviewoodinternationalauthor.co.uk

www.purityschoolofspirituality.co.uk

📞 **(+44)7787334044**

Ⓢ **Spiritualtherapist**

✉ **puritysos@outlook.com** or **purity2010@hotmail.co.uk**

> Michelle and I met on another book project. Her warrior spirit to never give up inspires me daily. Thank YOU, Michelle, for being a part of this project!
>
> **~ Aime Hutton**

CHAPTER 13

SOCIETY'S MISFIT

By Michelle E. Wood

I came home from work late to find my guests making my supper as their son sat and enjoyed a beer. I was not impressed! As we ventured to bed that night, I was pulling him up for his misgivings.

At 1:30 a.m., as I was about to give up and go to sleep, he announced my son was suicidal! My son announced this in front of our guests earlier that afternoon, yet no one felt the need to tell ME.

I had been home for five hours and now, at 1:30 in the morning, someone decided to tell me my son wanted to die. He didn't care whether he lived anymore.

I was mortified. To think this news came to me during an argument…

When I was pregnant with my son, I'd nearly lost him due to stress. He hated it when I had a bath. My baby bump would go ridged as I stepped into water. I found this strange but thought nothing of it.

When my son was born and I took him to the swimming pool, he would cling to me and scream continuously until we left the pool. This was very frustrating.

He struggled with feeding, becoming colicky. When he went onto solids, he struggled with eating and would quite often spit it out. This was also frustrating.

He was always slow to crawl and would cry often. He was slow at walking too. His behavior was intolerable. He would cling to me constantly.

By the time he was three years old, I couldn't cope any longer with his tantrums—he would hit, bite, and kick me. It got to the point my son would come downstairs in the morning and smash eggs on my kitchen floor, removing the shells, and wait for me to come down. He would watch me slip and fall on the eggs and laugh at me. I decided to go to the doctor and ask what was wrong with my son. My mum told me to check out his walk, because he kind of swung his hips.

One doctor said he needed discipline, another blamed my depression, and finally after a third opinion, my son was diagnosed with Perthes' disease—a condition where the hips do not form properly. His left hip was deformed, causing him immense pain.

This explained everything. I was riddled with guilt, tears streaming down my face as I got the news. After seeing the x-rays, I saw his left hip had no ball to his femur to fit into the socket in his pelvis, which had cysts forming over it.

He was medicated and this affected his eating habits. His behavior intensified and he had to be in a stroller until he was four years old.

School was the next stage for my son to challenge. He found he was very different from others and would try so hard to integrate with his peers, but he just seemed to antagonize them, which led to him being bullied. In Portsoy Primary School, his bullies got him to the point of no return and he wanted to die. He'd given up on living due to them bullying him because of his unique ways of thinking and acting. The school said they wanted the best for my son, but their answer was to get him psychiatric help—they even suggested he may have Asperger's syndrome.

We took their advice and took my son to a center that would diagnose him.

However, as the months went on, I found the more I focused on my son's needs the more settled he became. He didn't need a "label" that would be stuck to him for the rest of his life. So we no longer pursued the diagnoses.

We had changed schools three different times, and the same happened in two of these schools. At Macduff Primary School, his teachers said he was a problem and would segregate him to a table on his own. The children would find him either annoying or a target to bully.

He would often ask me to teach him myself at home, but at the time, I ran my own business fulltime as a beauty and complementary therapist, and I worried this would be difficult.

The third school we put him in specialized in children with difficulties and it was the only school in Scotland accredited with the autism Association. However, as he was leading up to go to high school, he became anxious again because he would have to face the bullies from both of his previous schools. That's how he became suicidal at the tender age of eleven years old!

We moved towns, with my work progressing into the healing and teaching world, and again my son asked me to teach him myself. I finally gave in and decided I needed to do what was best for my son because our relationship was being affected by his temperament. He was difficult and I was always on my guard, wondering what his mood was going to be that day. I was constantly in defensive mode.

Over the years, I worried our relationship could potentially end up the same way as my relationship with my mum. I was terrified. I didn't want my son to hate me. I was scared I would end up lashing back at him and lose control of myself as I struggled to understand what was going on with him. I refused to go where my mum had gone in my younger years.

I needed to help him but didn't know how. My relationship with my own mother was the same as when I was a child. How can I help him if my mum couldn't help me? How could I understand him when my mum couldn't understand me? I had no training in this field! I was a disappointment in my eyes and I pulled away from my son because of my own fears.

I was scared I would let him down as a parent! He reminded me of myself when I was his age. I too had felt different from my peers. I too was bullied at school. And I too became suicidal at the tender age of thirteen years old. History was repeating itself!

After many years of trauma, I came to realize that I needed to go within and find the answer to our situation…

I needed to find the answer so history had no place in our futures.

I found myself asking these questions:

What did I want from my mum when I was a child?

What would have made it better for me as a child?

The answer came—I needed to be loved and accepted just as I am! This is what I had been searching for to help my son!

I reduced my work load to part-time and started writing instead. I also took my children out of school. Now I homeschool them. My son and I get on really well now and his sense of wellbeing has turned around full circle.

All he needed was for me to love him and to tell him so, to accept him (the good, bad, and indifferent) and tell him so, and to listen to him and comfort him.

My advice to any parent is talk to your child as if you were a child too. Remember what like it was for you and what did you want then?

Chances are it will be the same for your child. The cycles will continue to rear their heads until we look within ourselves to find the answer to our very own needs.

After all, what works for one does not always work for another. We as humans are NOT a statistic. We are UNIQUE, each of us different in our very own ways.

As a parent, it is our duty to guide our children from a world of chaos into a place of love, harmony, and balance within our souls by listening, understanding, and loving them no matter how they turn out.

To see my son happy, no longer craving attention to the point of using negativity to get even was a pure blessing in itself.

Does your child NEED something from you? Are you LISTENING to their needs? Make the changes necessary today for all of your sakes. Our children are our future…

Inch by Inch

Jodi Tucker

If you were to say to me, "Tell me who you are without telling me what you do," I would answer that my personal purpose is to change the lives of the families I work with and their communities. Everything I do comes from that passion. As a clinician and advocate, I help people get from working hard and going nowhere to experiencing real change in their everyday lives. That's what matters! That's the theme for my business, my books, and my public speaking—empowering change.

Learn more about Jodi and how to reach her:

www.johncmaxwellgroup.com/joditucker

www.popexpert.com/jodi-tucker

www.kidsmattercanada.com

facebook.com/Kids-Matter-Inc

twitter.com/kidsmatter_inc

youtube.com/user/KidsMatterCanadaInc

Jodi and I met through eWomen Network. Her compassion to help others and help share their stories is why she is in this book. Thank YOU, Jodi, for being in this book with us!

~ Aime Hutton

CHAPTER 14

FIGHTING FOR CHANGE – MAKE A DIFFERENCE!

By Jodi Tucker

"The world is not dangerous of those who do harm but because of those who look at it without doing anything."

~ Albert Einstein

I have had the privilege of being introduced to Brooklyn and her family and supporting them on a journey that has touched parents and children across Canada and the world. Hers is a story of perseverance and fortitude—of one girl who chose not to be excluded and silent. It is a privilege to support such a passionate young woman.

In 2013, Brooklyn, a fifteen-year-old BC girl, was told she would be participating in an exchange program with a school in PEI, Canada. This was something Brooklyn had very much been looking forward to. You see, Brooklyn has autism and epilepsy. Sometimes her needs impacted her on a daily basis, sometimes not. For most people, Brooklyn's disability would have been invisible. Being included in a program that allowed her to meet new people and travel was a huge and exciting event! When Brooklyn's exchange began in BC in March 2014, she was delighted. Brooklyn had a partial complex seizure that had a devastating effect on the plans for her participation in the exchange program. The people in authority became frightened about how to support her and in response, Brooklyn was told she couldn't continue on with her classmates to PEI. She was kicked out for "not meeting the social mandate" of children who were participating. After Brooklyn began to raise issues about discrimination, Brooklyn's parents were told by organizers they could have Brooklyn go only if they recanted any statements about discrimination. When Brooklyn learned she would have to compromise her belief that she was no different than any other child, she refused.

Many individuals with disabilities[1] or medical issues face discrimination on a daily basis. The highest authority on disability in Canada comes from definitions provided by the World Health Organization (WHO). In May 2013, the World Health Assembly met to discuss the issues facing individuals with autism and reached a resolution that there must be "commitments to safeguard citizens from discrimination and social exclusion on the grounds of disability..."[2] Families and individuals with disabilities face this kind of environment on a daily basis. They are told, "When your disability is invisible and YOU are invisible, then you can participate." Brooklyn was told by her exchange organizers that maybe at a later time she would be a "suitable candidate" to participate. This would be no different than telling Rosa Parks that she could sit on a public bus when she was "less black." WHO reaffirmed the need to address the issues facing children with autism again in May 2014. Surprisingly, this authority on the issue of human rights has articulated exactly the circumstance Brooklyn found herself in.[3]

What impressed me the most about Brooklyn was the accuracy of her focus. Brooklyn's wish was to ensure this was not the experience of any other child. When systems and organizations do not have a clear line of authority, or accountability (in this case, there was neither), the result is a lack of process. This is called SYSTEMIC

---

[1] "Disabilities is an umbrella term, covering impairments, activity limitations, and participation restrictions. An impairment is a problem in body function or structure; an activity limitation is a difficulty encountered by an individual in executing a task or action; while a participation restriction is a problem experienced by an individual in involvement in life situations." (http://www.who.int/topics/disabilities/en/).

[2] http://www.autismspeaks.org/sites/default/files/images/b133_r1-autism_resolution_approved_by_eb133.pdf

[3] "The Health Assembly urged Member States to include the needs of individuals affected by autism spectrum and other developmental disorders in policies and programs related to child and adolescent health and development and mental health. " (http://www.who.int/mediacentre/news/releases/2014/WHA-20140523/en/)

DISCRIMINATION[4]. Brooklyn was able at age fifteen to identify this as the core issue. Brooklyn is calling for ACCOUNTABILITY[5]. In other words, the system or organization to ACCOUNT for process, decision-making criteria, and clear lines of responsibility. Anyone can say "we followed a process" BUT if they cannot demonstrate it through practice, they have indeed not been accountable for their actions. Brooklyn has not been disabled by her autism or epilepsy but by the structured ableism and lack of appropriate accountability demonstrated by the organizations involved in her exchange. Brooklyn and her family are giving a voice to an issue that impacts thousands of children across Canada.

Is there a procedure or a policy that governs how not-for-profit organizations and educators engage such issues? Indeed, there is. It's called the Canadian Charter of Human Rights. This is the law. It's not a suggestion to be applied at our convenience. It is based on our agreement with the United Nations about how human beings should be treated. It is based on the requirement that organizations be held accountable for how they make decisions. As I write this, there has been no demonstration of accountability from anyone, except Brooklyn and her mother, who shared honestly about Brooklyn's needs and who upheld the Canadian Charter of Human Rights in the face of great opposition.

When you have a disability, it fluctuates from day to day. This doesn't mean that your "health" has changed. Brooklyn having a seizure or two, or three, is NOT a change in "health" and is NOT a "health

---

[4] Systemic discrimination refers to patterns of behavior, policies or practices that are part of the structures of an organization, and which create or perpetuate disadvantage for racialized persons. It has a broad impact on an industry, profession, company, or geographic area. http://definitions. uslegal.com/s/systemic-discrimination/

[5] "Parties shall ensure that children with disabilities have the right to express their views freely on all matters affecting them, their views being given due weight in accordance with their age and maturity, on an equal basis with other children, and to be provided with disability and age-appropriate assistance to realize that right." http://www.ohchr.org/ EN/HRBodies/CRPD/Pages/ConventionRightsPersonsWithDisabilities. aspx#5

and safety issue." It means that she has what her mom shared with organizers in the beginning—epilepsy. It means they should have a coordinated response. It means they should treat her no differently than any other participant in this respect. Does health and safety mean that the days your child "doesn't look autistic" or "doesn't have a seizure" or "doesn't accidentally fall down in the gymnasium" are the only days they are safe to participate? Maybe that means none of our children are safe or healthy. People with disabilities have the same health needs as non-disabled people. They have the same rights to participate and define themselves in their lives as you or I. According to the First Report of Canada on the Convention of Rights of Persons with Disabilities, this applies to school, work, community, and individual expression[6].

True leadership is taking a stand that resonates from within you. It's not about your title or whether or not you get paid to show up. Brooklyn is a true leader. She understands the consequences of not stepping forward and she has vision for what can happen for others because of her story. From the beginning, she has understood her voice is not singular but represents many, many children across Canada. If only we had encountered that same commitment to leadership in her exchange organizers and teachers. If only they saw what Brooklyn sees and had stepped forward. Commentary about health and safety doesn't resonate—we parents have heard that before.

Empowerment is about POWER. It's not just a pep talk or a warm fuzzy feeling we get during the Hallmark card moments of our lives. EMPOWERMENT functions on the belief that there is enough power to share and that by giving people POWER, we have shared that power, not lost it. A scarcity mindset hoards POWER. This is DISEMPOWERMENT. When leaders or people in authority seek to gain power by hoarding it, they are functioning on the belief that there is only so much power to go around and that they can't give any away lest they run out themselves. Leadership is about serving others and recognizing that when you give power back, you have led others into a place that allows them to access their potential. Leaders

---

6 http://publications.gc.ca/collections/collection_2014/pc-ch/CH37-4-19-2013-eng.pdf

who EMPOWER understand that giving power to others increases outcomes not just in addition (you plus me) but it exponentially multiplies POWER. EMPOWERMENT, when it is done right, has the potential for infinite outcomes. This is where we get the POWER OF ONE. It just takes one person to share POWER to change the world... infinitely.

When you raise your voice and share your experience, you are empowering others to do the same. When you refuse to accept "good enough" or refuse to compromise your values, you are showing leadership. Your story is powerful—share it wide and far.

LINKS ABOUT BROOKLYN:

Brooklyn in the News:

podcast.cbc.ca/mp3/podcasts/maritimenoon_20140428_12828.mp3

www.theguardian.pe.ca/News/Local/2014-04-29/article-3705074/ Mother-of-B.C.-teen-with-disabilities-says-they-feel-harassed%2C-intimidated-by-P.E.I.-school-board/1

www.theguardian.pe.ca/News/Local/2014-04-29/article-3705511/ Autism-Society-hopes-for-resolution-between-B.C.-teen%2C-exhange-program/1

www.theguardian.pe.ca/section/2014-04-30/article-3707577/ Board%2C-school-fumble-badly-on-B.C.-teen/1

globalnews.ca/video/1305846/backlash-after-mission-teen-denied-pei-exchange-trip

www.missioncityrecord.com/news/257707101.html?mobile=true

www.troymedia.com/2014/05/04/a-textbook-case-of-how-not-to-do-things/

www.theguardian.pe.ca/Opinion/Letter-to-editor/2014-05-06/ article-3714335/School-board-must-provide-positive-influence-for-our-children/1

www.theguardian.pe.ca/Opinion/Letter-to-editor/2014-05-15/
article-3725881/Brooklyn-Mavis-continues-to-fight-back/1

Brooklyn's story and how to reach her:

youtu.be/_IpsH_-o_J4

twitter.com/Fight4Brooklyn

facebook.com/pages/Fight-Discrimination-with-
Brooklyn/554840391297399

LINKS ABOUT JODI:

Jodi in the news:

www.theguardian.pe.ca/Opinion/Letter-to-editor/2014-05-15/
article-3725881/Brooklyn-Mavis-continues-to-fight-back/1

www.abbynews.com/community/184442641.html

Lori Bothwell

Lori is a single parent of two exceptional boys, ages eleven and thirteen, whom she loves to taxi to rugby and hockey games. Lori and her boys—and two dogs—enjoy spending their summers camping in the Kootenays in BC, as well as hiking in the mountain ranges in local Kananaskis, Canmore, and Banff, Alberta. They enjoy sightseeing, skateboarding, going to movies, and walking their dogs together. "We enjoy working and playing together. As long as we're interacting, we can enjoy time together as a family." Lori loves yoga, reading, journaling, and Hula-hooping in her spare time.

Contacts:

✉ **loriebothwell@gmail.com**

f **facebook.com/loriebothwell**

Lori is a brilliant soul with a heart of gold. I am so excited to have Lori as part of this book project. Thank YOU, Lori, for your gifts of soul and spirit!

~ Aime Hutton

CHAPTER 15

IN THE SHADOW OF LOVE

By Lori Bothwell

When you're little, your shadow is fun to play with. As a child, the shadows were my playmates, full to stretch and mimic me. In school, I was often alone. Sometimes I stood there on the playground getting kicked in the back of my heels by my classmate, Cassey, until she got bored and went away. I was a fearful, timid child whom many did not understand. I was dreamy and spacey, as the adults would say. My cousins would call me stoned, and when I asked what that meant, they would roar with mocking laughter.

My five-year-old self was so free and happy—a time I still revisit to find that inner child to play with. She wore tattered, hand-me-down '70s cricket jeans with holes in the knees. She was wild and happy lying in the grass, picking lady bugs, or sitting up on the highest limb with her legs swaying back and forth as she sang songs to herself, sun glistening in her carrot-red locks. She was this sassy little girl who cut her bangs crooked in defiance and threw her mattress on the floor to protest a spanking. But she faded away like the sun does in late autumn, those tattered jeans replaced by a plaid skirt and pressed white blouse, her tousled windblown hair tamed into ringlets. I entered grade one and began to feel the coldness of conforming in a system where free spirit wasn't supported but was shamed and discouraged.

School became an institutional hell. The limbs of the aged, rough apple tree were replaced with a smooth, cool polished desk—the top of the desk swallowed by a gleaming yellow math book, smelling of mill paper. It was the size of a phone book to a six-year-old girl. Day after day, boredom settled in, stealing my passion.

I was labeled as having a learning disability. In grade three, I wandered in that dream state and sometimes walked up and down the rows of desks, copying my classmates work until, finally, my mom decided to switch me to another school. It was there that I came alive and stepped back into a world of art and imagination.

I finally had a teacher who would show me I had a place in this world of black and white pages and briefcases. Mrs. Vovan changed my whole world. I could see everything through the eyes of an artist. I was introduced to the world of poetry and realized all the symbols I used to make sense of this world could be translated into written form, or stanzas on a page. I chose the topic of fireworks and timidly walked up to her desk, asking for help and still carrying around the label of learning disabled. She asked me to close my eyes and describe what I saw and then, line-by-line, the page became a work of art, coloring the page. A passion for poetry and writing had been born. She would later publish my poem in a community bulletin. I fell in love with learning and worked so hard that year, dipping my fingers delightfully in paper mache, singing my heart out in school concerts while wearing a grass skirt.

Mrs. Vovan became a part of who I am today, as if she had mutated my artistic DNA forever to become the teacher I am today. I meet a lot of new students because I teach part-time as a substitute teacher. I love the thrill of meeting new students and learning new skills each day. I spread my joy of learning with the students I teach, and though I spend only a small amount of time with these students, I still establish a connection. My mission is to open their eyes to a bigger picture to what learning should be. I try to engage them and make it fun and share the message of self-acceptance and love. I am a picture of diversity, with crystals and medicine pouches hanging from my neck and a coat made of a tapestry—many different fabrics sewn together. I often take in a singing bowl and I'm always astonished at how the students light up with excitement as I play the tones for them with the mallet. I ask them what they think or feel after I play it and they tell me how calm or peaceful they feel afterwards. They also can't wait to try it, so I always make time for them to play the singing bowl, especially in classrooms I have visited previously because they expect I will bring the singing bowl with each visit.

I like to show the kids I enjoy teaching and learning with them and often demonstrate that I too like to color and play. One day, I brought in my Mandala coloring book and asked a few students who were also coloring if I could borrow some Crayola markers. I quietly returned to my desk and began coloring. I could see a buzz of curiosity was spreading, with excited little whispers and heads popping up from their pages on the desk, glancing in my direction. Several students came up afterward, offering their markers. I noticed suddenly all the students were deep into the creative expression of their coloring, and I encouraged the students to show their work to me and I shared my coloring with them. I enjoy participating with the kids. It's important for them to see adults can color too, so they know they can keep that inner child alive in them forever.

One of my favorite things to do with the kids, besides coloring, is to share my Hula-hooping. It's something I have been passionate about for three years. Hoopdance combines Hula-hooping and a free form of dance. I love to bring out the Hula-hoops whenever I teach Phys Ed. One day, the students had an obstacle course set up and were doing something known as "mission impossible." It's an obstacle course set up with balance beams, Hula-hoops, and other props so that the kids can move from one point to another without touching the ground. I grabbed an extra hoop from the course and started to Hula-hoop in the middle of the gym. I was waist hooping and dancing to the beat of the music, and before long I had a crowd of children watching me and grabbing hoops and diving right in. Soon they were showing me their own tricks and I helped them learn a few they were interested in.

One little boy became discouraged. I was able to show him how to rock his knees to keep the momentum of the hoop spinning. He squealed, "I did it!" and then proceeded to try it with three hoops!

I am always using opportunities like hooping to celebrate diversity. I especially love sharing the message of encouragement and acceptance with kids that mirror who I was when I met Mrs. Vovan.

One day, I saw a forlorn little blonde boy seated alone at the back of the class. My heart went out to this child, isolated and disheartened.

On his desk, taped in the right-hand corner, was a white note with **GET TO WORK** written in black Sharpie. I was disgusted and asked the nine year old if he felt that note helped him worked harder. He shrugged his shoulders, his eyes downcast in shame. I asked him if he would mind if I put a different note on top. He brightened and said sure. The new yellow sticky note read, **I AM A HARD WORKER!** Though I had been warned in the lesson plan about this student's behavior, I never encountered one behavioral incident; instead I had a perky, lively, and engaged student who had a beaming smile that could fill up a room!

We start off in this world exploring and pretending and thriving in a creative reality. To keep our inner child alive is to be alive. What we need is to play in our work, with our families, and with our partners every day. When we play, we connect to that space where everything is complete, and we discover joy and peace. I found that joy and peace thanks to Mrs. Vovan, who will forever live inside me. I take her with me every day when I teach children. For she is eternally young and will help me inspire and encourage children to embrace the little differences in themselves and find their true selves, so that the inner child lives on and on.

Hannelore, M.S.C., M.S.H.

Inspirational Story Teller, Author, Teacher, Motivational Speaker and Counselor.

Hannelore offers both public and corporate 'playshops' worldwide. She masterfully assists you to realize the brilliance of your full potential and power. She is dedicated to supporting others to manifest their greatest desires by tapping deeper into the realm of empowered thinking. Through her deep love and respect for animals and our beloved planet, she demonstrates techniques to awaken your understanding and respect for the innate intelligence of Nature.

Hannelore also facilitates her highly popular, 'Vision Crafting Wilderness Retreat' and the profoundly magical retreats, 'Communing with Dolphins', in which individuals engage in playful union with non-captive Dolphins in Hawaii.

www.Hannelore.ca

www.CommuningWithDolphins.com

Hannelore@Hannelore.ca

When Hannelore said yes to be in this book, I cried. I have been a fan of hers since 2001. It's a true honor to have YOU, Hannelore, in this book with us, sharing your amazing story of triumph over adversity of an amazing kind.

~ **Aime Hutton**

CHAPTER 16

SNAKES SHOVED DOWN MY BLOUSE AND SWASTIKAS CARVED ON MY DESK

By Hannelore, M.S.C., M.S.H.

"Why am I so ugly? Why does everyone hate me so much?" I was nine years old and it wasn't the first time I had to compose myself before returning to the classroom. Tears were streaming down my face. I stared at my reflection in the school's bathroom mirror. There was so much anguish in my eyes as I tried fixing my long braids, which were tousled having been grabbed and yanked by some of my classmates. I remember the physical pain and torment I felt in my heart as though it was only yesterday.

I was only three years old when my parents emigrated from Germany to a small community on the west coast of Vancouver Island. Ours was one of the first passenger ships to arrive in Canada shortly after World War II. We were definitely not welcomed by the town's anti-German community. In their innocence, the children quickly picked up on the hatred and prejudices of their parents. As I was old enough to start school, I discovered how deeply cruel children can be. I often found swastikas drawn in my books or carved on my desk. I was the last person chosen to be on someone's team, rarely if ever asked to play after school, and very reluctantly invited to a birthday party. I dreaded the school roll call every morning—it was always "Linda. Susan. Tom. Allan." Then "Hannelore." I would shrink down into my chair. All I heard was, "There she is, that horrible German!"

Our Saturday matinees at the community hall were often cowboy and Indian movies, with such stars as Roy Rogers, Dale Evans, and Gene Autry, but more often than not there were Nazi war movies. I dreaded those movies. In the other kids' eyes, I was one of those horrible Nazis. After the movies, the kids would form a circle around me, calling me names, punching and pushing me to the ground. An unfortunate garter snake would occasionally be shoved down my blouse. I could never understand the phrase "sticks and stones will break my bones but names will never hurt me." The sticks and stones physically hurt, but the name calling cut deeply into my heart and every fiber of my being. I often cried myself to sleep. A few times, my mother would hear me and insist I tell her what was wrong. She then met with their parents, which only made it worse, so I learned to stifle my sobs in my pillow case.

I spent much of my time playing on my own in the forest, where I created a fantasy world—a world where I could communicate and live in harmony with the animals, birds, and all of nature; a world where we were all at peace.

It was difficult for my mother, as well. After her third nervous breakdown, we moved back to Germany. Suddenly I was a celebrity — someone who came from the "wild west." For they too watched their cowboy and Indian matinees and were curious about this strange world I came from. I was surprised to find there were many genuinely nice and wonderful German people. It was here I had my first ever true friend. Her name was Rosel. I shared with her my pain and experiences of being bullied. We spent many wonderful long hours just talking. It was through her words of love and wisdom that I was able to view my situation in a different way. She prepared me for my return to Canada and taught me to have self-confidence, to not react or take personally the words and actions of the children around me, to do my best to ignore the taunts no matter how much it hurt. After a year in Germany, we returned to Canada. The bullying began right away. I held on to the words Rosel shared, and to my surprise, within a very short period of time, it magically stopped.

We moved from that small community later that year. Just in case, I changed my name from Hannelore to Lore. I did not realize it at the time, but I was burying my inner child by adopting a new identity — one that would hide the fact I was German.

I remember watching Sophie's Choice, starring Meryl Streep—a story of a woman who was sent to Auschwitz with her two young children.

She had to choose which one of her children would be gassed and which would be sent to a labor camp. I felt devastated by the horror of her dilemma! By now, I was aware that many countries throughout history committed genocide. But, as I was born a German, the shame and guilt of what the Nazis did to the Jews still remained as a dark shadow in my heart. How could humankind be so incredibly cruel?

Years—and several careers—later, I seriously embarked on my spiritual path. We were all asked to introduce ourselves at my Reiki Master class, when to my utmost surprise, I said: "My name is Hannelore." I had been Lore for over thirty years! In that moment, I felt the fear of persecution but realized it was time to reconnect with and claim my inner child.

Later that year, I was in New York City studying comparative religions and dimensions of physiology as part of my journey to become an ordained interfaith minister. It was here that a tremendous healing took place. We were at the completion of our first year, when, as part of the program, we were to share with the class something that impacted our lives. One of the students—Dinah, a Jewish middle aged woman—asked, "Who here is Jewish and who either survived the Holocaust or lost someone because of the Holocaust? " I immediately sank into my chair, once again feeling as I did when I was a young girl at school—the finger of shame pointed at me. She went on to say, "I thought I could never forgive that." What she said next surprised me. "I recently discovered, through a past life regression, that I was one of the SS officers who committed these atrocities."

After she completed sharing, an older German woman volunteered to speak next. She said, "I was twelve years old at the end of the war and one of many who stood outside the prison gates, ready to jeer at the Jewish prisoners when they were being released. When I saw their emaciated bodies, I realized we had been lied to. I spent the rest of my life doing what I could so that this would never happen again." Another German woman quickly raised her hand and shared, "I was born after the war but held onto the shame and guilt until my friend said to me 'Helga what are you doing—you look like a Holocaust Victim!'"

Later that morning, the three of us German women and a large group of Jewish people all shared our personal experiences—how we were all victims and how we took on various degrees of anger, hatred, blame, shame, and guilt. Through our sharing, we experienced such tremendous love and a profound act of release and forgiveness. The following morning, the woman who originally began sharing informed us that the rabbi was going to perform a "name change ceremony" for her. This was meant to be an emblem of healing and a sign of a bright new beginning. Witnesses were an important part of this ceremony. She asked the three of us to be her witnesses as she changed her name to "Eliana." The healing I felt take place not only impacted all of us in that room but reached out beyond time and space.

In that moment, the deep dark pain I carried in my heart all these years lifted.

When I finally understood the children who bullied me so many years ago, mirrored my own shame, I was able to release judgment of what happened in the war. Forgiveness does not mean to condone or to forget or to wish that the past could be changed. Instead, I choose to grow, to have compassion, and to offer a prayer of gratitude that I am not capable of that.

Mark Twain's words are carved in my heart: "Forgiveness is the fragrance that the violet sheds, on the heel that has crushed it."

As I look back on my childhood experiences, I now embrace these moments with gratitude. For it has taught me to have compassion for others and has given me strength and courage, not to mention, my tremendous love of nature. As Amma has so beautifully stated, "Nature is God made Visible." Nature encompassed me with her loving arms, drank in my many tears, absorbed my pain, patiently listened, and allowed me to surrender and discover *me*—a loving and sensitive little German girl.

Tanya Horne

Tanya Horne, better known in her circles as T, is a brilliant mother of three and a nurturing "mother" of countless more. Named the nurturer of soulful connections, she's consistently meeting new people and bringing them into the fold. T's energy is larger than life and she believes building community is best served through helping others. She remains dedicated to telling her story regarding sexual abuse, intending to shed light and create conversations on this subject. She is a coach, mentor, writer, friend, mother, leader, speaker, and program facilitator in the list of countless others.

www.tanyahorne.com

f **facebook.com/tanya.horne.73**

Tanya's tenacity is something I admire and is the reason she is in this book. She set the intention and made it happen. So honored and blessed to have YOU, Tanya, in this project!

~ Aime Hutton

CHAPTER 17

SHADOW DANCING WITH SEXUAL ABUSE
By Tanya Horne

September 27, 2003, seemed a day like any other—get ready, feed the kids, and leave for work. I quickly came to understand it was a day that would become infamously branded in the depths of my soul. This day would alter the trajectory of my life's path forever.

My son, fourteen, came into the consignment shop where I worked. He was visibly shaken and I couldn't put my finger on it, but I could sense something was seriously wrong. He just kept repeating, "I don't want to break your heart." The words which crossed his lips would in fact shatter my heart. They would be the most horrific thing I had ever heard. He uttered the words, "My dad comes to visit me in my room at night." The room started spinning in slow motion and we crumbled to the floor in a pile of devastation. Writhing in pain, engulfed in the moment of deep wounds, shattered dreams, pain, anger, disbelief, rolling around like helpless wounded animals waiting to be put out of misery. Sadly, I understand first-hand the daunting task of being a sexual abuse victim and how it has shaped my life and my choices. Now, as a mother, and a passionately protective one, I was to face what that meant to my children, to my marriage. Nothing could have ever prepared me to hear and respond to this type of tragedy. Instantly, I was crippled with fear, riddled with guilt and shame of not being able to protect my children from the plight of sexual abuse. Sorrow so deep it felt like dying might offer the only reprieve.

The world seemed bleak and dark at best. I had to confront my husband and then turn him into the police. My heart was broken and the depths of my sorrow were immeasurable. I powered through, knowing I had three children I was responsible for.

Life is a process and my lesson has been how to grieve when I feel sad, find appropriate outlets for my anger, and learn to respond from a place of love. These are all things which have taken conscious effort and intention; they are part of my practice. Navigating life over the past ten years has had its fair share of challenges, defeats, and victories. I remember thinking, *There's no way I will ever smile again, laugh again, trust again.* I have come to find that there are pockets of joy, reasons to smile, to laugh again. In order to heal, I have had to continually be willing to be conscious of my thoughts, my choices, and my actions. To lead my children through each of their own experience(s) within this tragedy. I have had to learn how to own my actions and reactions.

More than ten years after the fact, I take time to celebrate my accomplishments, as I know sometimes sexual abuse can turn into a life sentence of self-destructive behaviors, drug abuse, and repeating cycles of abuse—to name just a few. I have come to understand and believe in harnessing the power of intention. Intention is driven by the outcome I would like to create. Consistently seeking to create healing and wellness for myself, my children, and my family has remained my focus. My experiences have taught me that hate ignites more energy of abuse. It gains power through shame and guilt associated with the famous "we don't talk about these kinds of things" way of dealing with those experiences, only breeding more hate. These responses, of course, lead to bitter cycles of further abuse, feeding the shadow abyss which has been allowed to grow and dominate so many victims' lives. Healing can only happen truly when love is embraced and embodied. My belief is that love is rooted in faith and the alternative is fear, which continually builds further mistrust, anger, and resentment. Resentment potentially becomes a self-limiting prison where anger and hostility flourish.

I spent the first year trying to keep these things under wraps. I became bitterly aware of the tragic heaviness and price of carrying this burden. Shame and guilt fueling and navigating, blindly forging, furthering the abuse cycle which thrives under the cover of dark silence. A life filled with fear, limitations, patterns of low self-esteem, avoiding feelings, and unintentionally perpetuating abuse.

Shame is abuse turned inwards. It is a generational burden handed down through families worried about what people will say or what will they think? Dirty little secrets satisfying the endless voracious hunger of abuse. Despair is often felt in those moments of being and feeling all alone. The constant brain banter questioning of why? Why did this happen to me? What did I do to deserve this? Is there something wrong with me? Am I damaged goods? All the questions which burdened my mind in the quest to make sense out of the senseless. Sadly, statistics boast sexual abuse is ever so prevalent a problem and a continuously growing concern. Yet most people want to shove it where it will never see the light — a hostage to the darkness, going on with life, ignorant to the insidiousness of abuse when left to fester.

Forgiveness is a cherished gift I give to myself. Often people misinterpret forgiveness to mean that forgiving somehow makes the action/behavior OK. Love and acceptance are the only way I have created true healing and helped aid my family in our journey. The alternative, where I have expended huge amounts of energy over the past ten years, is to feel so agitated, so angry and resentful, that it spews forth, dictating and enforcing the venomous nature of abuse. Resistance and anger fueling the very thing I say I don't want. It is a fine line, and for me it has been a practice.

My intention is to continue to talk about it, regaining ownership over my power and allowing my voice to brave the message of love. As I begin to utilize my voice to carry this message of hope, I encounter so many others who subscribe to the idea that it is best left unsaid. *Unsaid* allows the silence to gain power and control, dictating the limitations and shackles that I so often surrender to as my only choice. I am here to inspire change in the area of sexual abuse, to shed my light in hopes of inspiring others to do the same. The silence screams in the shadows, away from sight, where it delights in the idea of its gaining power. I believe my voice is best used in support of the possibilities of change, to create conversations which will eventually eliminate the shadow(s). Even though talking about it often makes people uncomfortable in the awkwardness of the subject, I believe it is vital. The thought that it makes people uncomfortable is maddening to me,

I want to know why more people aren't outraged about constantly raising statistics which easily morphs into other forms of abuse?

 I choose to re-frame this tragedy as an opportunity to create change so others going forward may be saved from the burden(s) of abuse. My legacy for my children, myself, and my community is to see love prevail, root, and grow, to end abuse cycles in my genealogy, and to aid others to facilitate the same for theirs. Being a survivor is not enough. I then live at the effect of their twistedness and poor choices instead of at the cause of my purpose, my dreams, my deepest desires. I stand for cultivating, growing, and nurturing the idea of thriving. I believe thriving is the only way to actually thwart the nature of abuse. "It" can become an identity. "It" becomes a driving force which unintentionally controls how I end up living my life. "It" can only live if I allow it to continue. I am not responsible or at fault for being abused. I am, however, responsible for how I deal with it. How I allow it to carve out my limitations and ultimately dictate my future is really up to me. It is a choice: to remain the victim or to choose to thrive.

Love is the answer. Loving support has been vital for me staying the course when so many moments of despair have often taken me out. I am dedicated to practicing love, acceptance, and forgiveness, aiding the intention of cultivating further healing. Encouragement and loving support continue to play active roles in returning to my heart, to leading with love.

If you have been abused, *tell*. Tell until someone pays attention and offers you the help that you need. It is never OK, ever. It is never your fault, ever. You deserve the chance to heal. You deserve the opportunity to put an end to abuse cycles. Step into the light and raise your voice. You have been silent long enough.

Mady Horne

Madysen is a seventeen-year-old student in eleventh grade. She has a voracious appetite for books. Madysen is an aspiring photographer and writer. She desires to bring about change in the world through sharing her story. Drama is one of her favorite classes and she loves to be boldly animated in front of her friends, sometimes looking a fool. Her aspirations are to work in a library, travel the world, and hopefully write and take photographs on her travels. Her love for rainbows is evident in her space(s). She is very thankful for this opportunity to share her story.

Madysen is the daughter of Tanya. She is so brave and strong. I am so honored to have you, Madysen, be a part of the book with your mum!

~ Aime Hutton

CHAPTER 18

TAKING BACK MY CONTROL

By Mady Horne

I have two siblings—my brother, Kam, and my sister, Ryleigh. We all have different fathers, but I consider them my full siblings, as we grew up in the same house. I am the youngest, and my father is the one that stuck around. Even though he wasn't their real father, we all called him dad, and were, for all intents and purposes, a loving family. He loved us, he was funny and witty, and he was the best dad ever—my dad. Then he made some incredibly horrible decisions that ripped our family apart.

I was too young to grasp precisely what was happening, but it still hit me like a ton of bricks. I could sense, but not yet comprehend, the devastation that was ripping through my family. All I knew was that my dad was suddenly gone. My world as I knew it would never be the same. I came to realize as I grew older that my family was irreparably broken. My father chose to go down a dark path by molesting my brother and sister. Following my brother's disclosure, my mom insisted that my father turn himself in to the police. I remember the confusion of seeing my father walking away, but I could sense and feel that something was not right. I can call to mind the feeling of my nana pulling me away as I was wailing for my father. Recalling a feeling of great inner turmoil, just weeping and feeling lost in the whirlwind of raw emotions flooding from my family.

Fathers are supposed to be loving, protective—they're supposed to never let any wrong happen to you. They are supposed to guide you through the hardships and woes that life will inevitably throw at you. Although my dad taught me how to ride a bike, to hike, to camp—by making the decisions he did, he ultimately failed me and my whole family.

I watched as my mom's light and spirit dimmed,. I saw my sister and brother smash into pieces. I was crushed. I felt like I didn't deserve to hurt like them. It didn't happen to me, so why should I be hurting so much? I carried tremendous amounts of shame and guilt because he was my father, I was *his* daughter, and how could they ever love me the same after what he did to them? I went through too many instances where I hated myself for what he did to them. I felt like I was broken beyond repair, and it was wrong for me to feel that way.

My mom and brother's relationship was rocky at best. I experienced many fights, and the atmosphere was often tense. It wasn't long after the tension became unbearable that my brother moved out of the house at the tender age of sixteen. I witnessed my sister hurting herself physically, mentally, and emotionally. I vowed that I would never do that to myself. In the long run, I did it unintentionally. I locked myself away. I didn't let my true light shine because I thought I was just some pedophile's daughter who didn't deserve the unconditional love and acceptance that was flowing freely from my damaged family. I became a recluse; I read books by the dozen and never ventured far from home. I've never thought of hurting myself or killing myself, but I've often thought it would be so much easier if I had never *been*. I felt I was inadequate. I felt I was there adding more pain, stoking the ever-growing fire.

I now know that my pain was and remains as important as theirs, as anyone's. I don't believe that someone's pain is more or less than someone else's. It took me years to recognize and understand it. Just because "it" didn't happen to me doesn't mean that I don't have the right to acknowledge my damage, my aching, and my pain. I had my own experience within this catastrophe. I might not understand the pain that people experience when it happens directly to them, but I did see it firsthand with my brother and sister. For years, I blamed my mom, and for no reason. But at one point in my life, I had a revelation. My mom, my beautiful, eccentric, strong, *amazing* mom is the person who kept my family whole. She sacrificed everything to make sure that my siblings and I would be all right. It took me years to believe everything my family was telling me; that I mattered, that they loved me purely and wholeheartedly, and that they didn't blame me for what happened.

I want people to know that it is fair to hurt. That it's OK to rest in the feelings, to sift through them. Sometimes it is challenging to confront the feelings for the fear of not knowing if it will turn out all right. Healing is the act of choosing to pull myself up, to change my life, and stop living like the victim, effectively taking my life back. It has been challenging but I haven't let the fact that my *father* is a pedophile rule and control my life. I know that if this situation hadn't happened, I would not be the same person that I am today. I wouldn't be going in the direction that my life story is going. I would most likely be damaged beyond repair, with self-destructive behaviors ruling my choices. I still go through tremendous rough patches where I just don't understand why something like this would ever happen to me. I know that by having this experience, and talking about it, I am lending my voice to the cause that will help others pull through the darkness and desolation, and say, "**You may be able to affect me now, but you will *never, ever* control me**." I got through everything with the help of books and my loving, amazing family. Family to me doesn't just mean blood; family is whoever you deem worthy of your love and trust.

I know some people might be thinking: what does this seventeen year old even know? She's just seventeen. My life dictated me having to grow up before my time, and I'm not saying I am some genius, like Leonardo da Vinci, but I do have some wisdom that I feel should be shared. I have been through monumental hardships; I have been given an opportunity to shed my silence and talk about it, helping people in the process. I believe that the sharing of my story is tremendously valuable to my healing, hopefully helping others, and giving them strength to carry on.

I hope you all take a moment and just revel in love. Breathe it in and out. I believe that love is the answer. If you believe that there truly isn't someone out there who loves you (and I know it may sound cliché), know that I love you. Love, just pure love, is the best healer. Embracing love has been the only path I have found which leads to a life of happiness and fulfillment.

Dianna Watson

Dianna is a freelance writer, holistic healer, entrepreneur, speaker, musician, and global traveler. She offers holistic healing services in her home town of Kelowna, BC, and abroad. Since May 2013, she has been co-facilitating group spiritual gatherings that coincide with her business of inspiring the feminine energies to blossom. Dianna has traveled through sixty countries and has authored many travel-related publications. She also writes poetry, spiritual magazine articles, and has been a member of Toastmasters International for eight years. Dianna loves to engage in joyful activities, such as playing in a band, dancing, and swimming with dolphins.

Dianna can be reached at:

✉ **iamdiannaw@gmail.com**
f **Dianna Watson Kelowna**

Dianna and I met through Hannelore (another author in this book). Her spirit and wisdom can be felt even on the phone. Thank YOU Dianna for being a part of this book project with us!

~ Aime Hutton

CHAPTER 19

RISING UP FROM THE DARKNESS

By Dianna Watson

"I feel like I'm drowning in a deep dark hole and I don't know how to get out!" Have you ever found yourself lost in such a deep darkness? I knew this dismal place well in my early teens, and through this learning journey I discovered indispensable ways to rise up from this darkness.

I was fortunate to grow up in a small town in northern Ontario, Canada, with Mother Nature all around me. As a curious, precocious child, I often found myself drawn to stone treasures and fascinating plant and animal discoveries within this alluring world that existed just outside my door. Nature was my BFF (best friend forever), and some days it felt like my *only* friend.

My family dynamics often felt stressful and overwhelming for me. I lived with three other siblings—all a year apart, an alcoholic father, and a mother who had few tools to cope with the everyday challenges before her. Thankfully, she instinctively gave us a lot of love in the best way she knew how. When I was old enough to recognize we had less than others in our community, I felt embarrassment and shame at our limited belongings and restricted opportunities. My instinctive response to the disturbing verbal outbursts, a father who didn't do well as a provider, and modest financial limitations was to withdraw into my shell. I was often referred to as "shy" and "very quiet."

One place I knew I could find solace was outside in the forest near our home. No one placed any demands on me while I was there. I found a deep peace that enveloped me like that nurturing hug I longed for. I could simply be me, and I felt completely accepted just as I was. In this safe haven, there were no rules or expectations, no criticisms, no disorder, crises, or chaos. All was balanced, harmonious, quiet, and deeply peaceful. Nature was my safe sanctuary, personal theatre stage, inspiring science classroom, and my natural playground. The trees were my allies and my confidants. The small animals, insects, and birds were my best friends, for I spoke to them and they kept my secrets safe. I could relate to John Burroughs when he said, "I go to nature to be soothed and healed, and to have my senses put in order."

As I grew up, I felt different from other children. I wasn't interested in playing with dolls like my younger sisters. I wanted to be outside playing cowboys and Indians with my older brother, for he was often playing in the forest. I recognized my uniqueness when my classmates would dress in the same style and engage in activities because the others were doing it. In my peerless and unique way, this gave me the clue to do the opposite. I knew early on I was certainly not a sheep yet couldn't figure out where or how to fit in. I felt like a butterfly, anxiously waiting to emerge from its dark cocoon. I was very lonely as I walked this path of being labeled "a weirdo." Yet in some bizarre way, this felt like a compliment to me.

In my early teens, I eventually bonded with a couple of girls who appreciated my individuality and love of nature, for we mirrored each other. They became an important part of my socializing stage and we shared many dreams and joyous times together. They often had fewer boundaries and later deadlines to return home compared to me, and I would sometimes ignore my curfew and stay out later than what was asked of me. My mother's discipline of choice was to ground us. I could not go out for a specified length of time, except to attend school. This time was very hard on me—a true punishment indeed. I felt a deep longing within me for that precious time playing with those few friends I had become so connected with. My greatest challenge during those confinement days was not being able to be with my nature friends in the nearby forest.

When I would break curfew, it was my strong need to reconnect with my outside stimulation and joy that overruled the repercussions of not obeying authority. My passion for freedom that welled up from deep within drove me to break out of this prison-like existence. The grounding restrictions got longer. My mother probably didn't know how else to enforce her rules. It became too crushing on my free spirit, feeling very alone without those outward connections that brought out my zest for life. I eventually shut the clam shell so tightly that depression finally overcame me. My world was dark; the stories I ran in my mind were very negative because that was all I saw around me. My school work began to suffer and my joy for life was a mere distant memory. At one point, I kept a journal handy because I always loved to write. In those days, we called it a diary. Do you remember those little books with a lock and key so no one else would be able to read your secrets?

I still remember it well. My little red diary held many of my deepest secrets concealed inside, mirroring the feelings that remained locked within my heart. Like a true friend that would never betray you, and with whom I could share everything, this diary became my lifeline. I wrote about my anger at being deprived of what brought me joy, my frustrations and hopelessness of not being able to do anything about it or our unfortunate family lifestyle, and my self-condemnation for having made poor choices that put me in that dire position. My diary heard me spill out my guts about how I desperately needed to get out of this restrictive environment.

I also poured out my longing for freedom and my desire to reconnect with nature and my girlfriends. I knew I deeply wanted those uplifting joyous feelings back. Eventually those distant feelings that "all was right with the world" came flowing back into my heart. I truly believe there was some angelic intervention that came through those writings to help me recognize I had to do something differently in order to return to what brought me fulfillment and happiness. Today, I understand how this journaling was the critical catalyst for the lifeline that drew me out of my depression.

As I rose up from that darkness, I came to understand that my mother, out of love for me, was doing her best to ensure I was kept safe and well. I finally realized that if I followed her guidelines, I could once again return to the precious things that brought me such joy and revive my passion for life once again. This was a huge turning point for me, and as you could imagine, brought such relief from my mother as well. *Anaïs Nin* expressed my shift well: "And the day came when the risk to remain tight in a bud was more painful than the risk it took to blossom."

Today, I can appreciate the many benefits of journaling. I have always found this form of writing very helpful in allowing my thoughts to easily flow, like having a witness to what I'm thinking. I see journalizing as words privately shared between me and the paper in front of me. It continues to provide me with the clarity to understand my past, present, and future. Through this understanding, I now know my father did the best he could. Journaling helps me gain a better connection with my values, emotions, and goals. From this clear place, I can more easily problem solve. As a result, the budding writer in me has blossomed, I have become more creative, and this method of communication has become the best means to express myself. As I come to know myself more deeply, my comfort in speaking out constantly improves.

My love for Mother Nature not only continues to this day, but I feel the connection deepening as I recognize the many blessings She offers us when we're open to seeing them. I am fascinated by the changes in all life forms each season, the balance and harmony that Mother Nature expresses in so many varied colorful ways, and the deep peace that pervades in the stillness the forests hold. I love Hal Borland's description: "Knowing trees, I understand the meaning of patience. Knowing grass, I can appreciate persistence."

No matter how dark things might look, there is always a light somewhere to guide you to a solution. It helps to have tools, such as journaling, and to know Mother Nature is always there to support you, provide the space, and be the silent witness for change to unfold.

Inch by Inch

Dennise C. Neilson

Dennise is an outstanding intuitive healer, Reiki master, holistic therapist, counselor, writer, poet, gifted player of the Native American flute, and Blog Talk Radio show host for The Two Spirits Connection with The Sacred Tree of Life.

Additional studies include psychosomatic therapy, power of intuition module 1, power of intuition certified training, the power of intuition advanced training, and the mirrors of relationships. Dennise has also assisted in the power of intuition training for nine years.

Dennise is a recording artist with her Native American flute.

Dennise also makes beautiful bead work that she learned while working at the Blackfoot Art Gallery.

Dennise and I have only known each other for a short time, but I knew her story was powerful and would help so many other families with children going through the same situation. Thank YOU, Dennise, for being in this book project!

~ Aime Hutton

CHAPTER 20

UNDERSTANDING THE DIVINITY OF ONE'S OWN SELF

By Dennise C. Neilson

I am a transgendered Two Spirit.

Even at the early age of eight months, I understood we are born such intelligent beings, created that way by our Creator. Hidden from us is the knowledge of who each of us truly is. Lies are fed to us, numbing us down. Yet there has always been a few of us that have held to our contract and followed through by setting the example of how each of us is to be true to our higher self.

I am a transgendered Two Spirit, born in a male body, yet always wanting to be a girl. I grew up with no one to talk to about whom and what I felt I truly was. It would be forty-three years later before I would come across the information that would free me. The day the female aspect of me would finally be able to see the light of day, on a continual basis. The closet was being torn down—no more hiding. Yet the self-abuse would still continue for a few more years. Some of that self-abuse had drifted over into the family that I had helped raise with my wife of twenty-five years. This is one of the unique connections we have to one another, our connection to all that is around us. In one form or another, we all have a closet to break out of, a closet to tear down, to find the self-love of being a perfect creation. In perfection, we experience many imperfections. This is one of the ways each of us discovers our true essence.

As I would speak at a very young age, just being me, I noticed people would be uncomfortable with what I said. Even my actions of playing with a doll brought out the uncomfortable feelings in people. When a group of kids got together in the community that I was living in, I was excluded and lied to. I was told there was not enough room, for me. The blatant self-evident truth that there was room for me made me wonder why they were being so mean. Being different in their eyes, being different from what they had been taught—somehow that made me look freakish to them.

That is how I felt with the attitudes they put out toward me. Sticks and stones may break the bones, or even kill us. Attitudes, lies, and gossip—they leave permanent emotional scares. So to survive life, I learned at an early age to adjust, hide, blend in—to be like others. Doing all this at the expense of not being true to myself. When one is not true to their own self, the guilt brings on so much self-abuse and breeds the disdain of not liking yourself. I am supposedly of Divine origin, just like everyone else. Where else would we come from? We are either of Divine origin, or we are genetically created by scientists. Or we are adopted into Divine origin through certain ceremonies.

In each of us there is a built-in system that says, "I will live at all costs. I must stay alive." If you could only understand how many times I would think of just ending my life. In my teenage years, it was Saturday when everyone was gone to town. That's when the girl would come out. Such joy being in the light, out of the closet. Five or six beautiful hours going through my mom's closet. Then just before the family got home the girl would reluctantly give up and go back to being in the closet, away from the light, back in the darkness. The rest of the week would be the beating-myself-up ritual, vowing to never do this again. Then Saturday rolled around again, and the girl was beating at the closet door, wanting her dress on, wanting the feminine to be in the light. Out she would come for a few more hours. And the next the cycle of abuse would start all over again, another round of self-abuse. As I write this, I see that I was very much involved in a marathon of self-abuse—years of self-abuse. It was all verbal abuse. I look at this now, and wow, I am still here writing this. I have survived.

It was in 1997 when I first got on the Internet. I pull up the word *cross-dresser*. I was so amazed to find there were so many like me. I was not a lonely freak—one of a kind. There were others, many others, like me. Creator was with me all the way on this search. I found nothing but beautiful uplifting people that were grounded to the source of life. All I did was research, read, and talk. Wow. Yet something was still not right. Something was missing. I remember the day so well. The day I found out about the Two Spirit people. Thank you, Wendy Susan Parker for that article on the Two Spirit people. We were highly revered in the tribes as healers, counselors, therapists, Shamans, and witch doctors, highly sought after for our abilities in those areas. We were also called the third gender. It was the first time in my whole life I was actually excited about me. This started the creation of the journey. Creating in my heart the role of a Two Spirit. Two Spirits are usually taught the ways by elders. I had no elders to teach me. So I connected with my heart. I listened to my heart. I worked at being a Two Spirit. Speaking it, walking it, living it.

As a boy, I lived that life good; I had to, being raised on the farm. I can only imagine how much better life would have been if I would have had the freedom to be all of me. I learned at an early age how to blend in—it was more important to be safe and alive. There really is a difference between acting out a life and living a life. There are days I still long to be a full genetic woman with a moon time. I guess there may be a magical transference one day when I have life all together. So in the meantime, I work each day being me, embracing me. As a one teacher taught me:

I embrace this man

I embrace this woman

I love this man

I love this woman

I express this man

I express this woman

For I am both man and woman.

I am a Two Spirit. We two spirits are gifts from Creator. We are gifts to humanity. It has not been an easy walk for me, yet I am still here.

May we all walk our path with dignity. For each of us is connected to all that is around us—through the Delta 10 Mitochondrial DNA.

It is time for all abuse to be done and all women, children, males, spouses, and all forms of transgendered people stop hurting each other, themselves. This is when I learned that when I notice myself with respect, others would notice me with respect too. This is how we break the cycles of abuse—when we all start respecting the essence of our own life. That is when this Mother Earth will make her shift. We are an extension of Mother Earth. What we do to ourselves and others, we do to her. Why would we harm our mother? Why would we harm ourselves?

To all my relations, love yourself.

Inch by Inch

128

Tara Tierney

Tara Tierney is an international bestselling author, blogger, and poet. She is currently working on a series of children's books and an autobiography. Tara is devoted to learning how to be her authentic, best self, and through this journey she sings karaoke every chance she can—even at home with her cat as the audience! Visit her blog at www.taracle.com.

Tara and I met on another book project. Tara is spunky, awesome, and can bounce back from anything. Thank YOU, Tara, for being in this book project with us!

~ Aime Hutton

CHAPTER 21

FROM HOPELESSNESS TO PROMISE
By Tara Tierney

I was the single mother of a boisterous but shy daughter who could light up my life with a smile and bring me to tears with hers. Shawna always had a hard time making and keeping friends but was always concerned for the feelings of others. The problem was she had always been bullied for being heavier than all the other kids—and worse, she believed what they said.

When she was eight, I fell in love with a man who lived in the Netherlands and chose to move us overseas while Shawna was young. We were to move on September 11, 2001, but a week prior, I postponed to September 18. After the events of 9/11, I knew changing the move date was a sign it was meant to be. So, I swallowed my fear and boarded an overseas flight with nothing but my daughter and our suitcases, to live in Holland.

Life in a foreign country was fantastic! Climate was different, we had a different language to learn, and there were a lot of new experiences and people in our lives. For the first time in her life, I could take Shawna to school, have her home for lunch, and pick her up after school. Shawna started school immediately and was immersed in to class, learning to speak Dutch instantly. She was fluent within six months!

Soon after moving, I realized I was becoming depressed (this would be my second bout with the illness). I wasn't making any friends and spent my days riding my bike on my own or staying at home crafting and Internet-chatting with other Canadians living abroad. Life became a regular pattern with no new surprises—unfulfilling. I am an extremely social person but I was becoming a hermit. And, although outwardly a person couldn't tell, I knew Shawna was unhappy and she hadn't made friends.

She was being bullied at school. I never thought this would happen where we made our fresh start! Holland was supposed to be liberal; very tolerant. Not when it came to immigrants. There was a huge immigration problem, and it did not seem to matter what country a person came from—some people thought newcomers still didn't belong. And this translated over to their kids. Add the fact that Shawna was slightly bigger than the other kids (taller and weight), and she was perfect fodder for the horrible behavior of others.

The first Christmas, in an attempt to have Shawna participate and fit in, I was getting her ready for a school event. I had hope that this would help her to be liked, so I was anxious to get everything right but I decided to try something new with her hair. This turned out to be the worst mistake I could never have imagined. I got a round brush tangled on the very first piece of hair and it was right on the top of her head. As anxiety settled in, my panic level increased exponentially. It was tangled so badly, but to cut it out would ruin her hair. I began crying uncontrollably and totally freaked out. I kept apologizing to Shawna and she kept repeating to me "It's OK, Mom. It's OK," with a look of concern on her little angelic face.

We were now late for the school function. Thankfully, my husband, Marcel (who must have been completely shocked at the spectacle), was able to contact a hairdresser to help but ultimately the brush had to be cut out. Shawna was completely traumatized (more from my behavior, less about her hair), but I was still intent on getting her to the school although the function was now almost over. She no longer wanted to be anywhere *near* the school; I wouldn't hear of it…Yes, I made her go. We dropped her off and my poor shocked husband picked her up after.

How Shawna was ever able to trust me again is a mystery. I could no longer trust my emotions myself. Shawna became increasingly unhappy and my depression turned into an OCD-type need to control my environment. It was during this time I discovered that my fear reaction to anything was anger.

131

Once, Shawna was riding her bike to school and I was walking with her. We were both having a decent, possibly good, day. The small path to her school was bordered on either side with nettle bushes—they have thorns that are a cross between rose thorns and fiberglass—and she lost balance and fell over on her bike directly on them. She was screaming in pain and surprise, and I lost it. I started screaming at her to get up and get moving, dammit! She was crying, telling me she needed help up. I grabbed her arm and her bike with rage and told her to stop crying, smarten up, get to school, and stop whining! She got up, limped down to school, and I knew I had just become a monster and felt helpless to control it.

Around the fall of our second year there, Shawna became so depressed, we knew we needed help and intervention before something irreversible happened. We found counseling for her, which was helping a little, but she was still far from OK. Marcel was becoming disenchanted with his job and worried about Shawna and me. The next spring, we decided to pack up and move back to Canada.

But after a year home and still the target of school bullying, Shawna's birth father, my stepfather, and my grandfather all died within one month of each other—two were sudden and a complete shock. Shawna now had abandonment issues that ran very deep, all tangled with the pre-teen emotions of guilt, added to feeling unloved. She started counseling and we all worked together just to make it through.

As a teen, she was so empathetic she was taking on the worries of all of her friends. When I didn't know what to do or say, I asked her to call the Kids Help Line—they may have more ideas or solutions that I hadn't thought of and they are trained to help her. She utilized this resource a few times and it proved to be one of the best parenting decisions I had ever made.

During and since high school, Shawna received counseling from a psychologist, as did I. I separated from Marcel in 2011, much to the surprise of all of us. I hadn't been happy for a long time and left, which meant leaving Shawna as well. Marcel and I worked well together, even throughout the separation, and we continue to be best friends. We are proud to be a positive example of remaining friendly during relationship struggles.

Shawna, Marcel, and I have been painfully honest with each other regarding our feelings and discussing our lives during our stay in Holland. Marcel and I were shocked to hear Shawna admit that she felt so hopeless in Holland, that she had planned her own suicide by knife so it would happen at school where she was so horribly treated. She was ten! She prefers not to think of that time and has almost completely lost her knowledge of Dutch. We are so glad we moved and still remain a strong family unit, I'm glad to say.

Since leaving, I have embarked on some serious personal development work, and I can truly say I am the happiest person I have ever been, discovering facets of myself that I once knew but forgot and am living my truth as a loving, giving and caring woman. I have also been diagnosed as bipolar II and am receiving therapy through medication and a psychiatrist.

Because of the transformation I've been making, and working with my daughter to pay forward the teaching I have received, Shawna is now at the best place in her own life. She has confronted me with the resurfacing of her abandonment issues due to my leaving, and I have discussed many of my parenting shortfalls and apologized for some of it (only some!). Our relationship has never been better.

Shawna has very recently flourished — recognizing and accepting her talent, beauty, and wisdom. Her relationships are healthy, she's accepted her passion to be her vocation, and most importantly, she now believes in herself and her worth. As a parent, it's been an honor to be on her journey with her and to see her thrive in all aspects of her life. I'm excited to see how far she's going!

I love you, Shawna, and am so proud of the person you are — body, mind, and soul.

Lesson to pay forward: As a parent, be courageous enough to recognize and admit when you need help. We cannot all be "super parent," but we can be super brave by facing the unknown and asking for help. Speak with your family doctor about counseling options, utilize the

Kids Help Phone (for teens as well), ask for advice from your local health network. You'll be glad you did.

Kids Help Phone

1-800-668-6868

KidsHelpPhone.ca

Hilary Davis

I arrived in Canada many years ago, having grown up in Dublin, Ireland. I have four grown children and four grandchildren. I was a single mum who returned to school and fell in love with learning. I have numerous business courses, certificates, and a degree in education. I have written text books, curriculum, and computer programs for teachers. I am now a retired high school teacher who fills her days with painting, reading, writing, and volunteer-teaching English to Mexican children in the village of my winter home. I love to travel and I'm always ready for new adventures.

Contact Hilary:

✉ hd.ebizglobal@gmail.com

Find more out about Sonny here:

✉ sonnyandchair@gmail.com

f facebook.com/pages/Contentment-is-Wealth-Harmony-Integration/154050408113147

g+ plus.google.com/u/0/105885298336597591381

in ca.linkedin.com/pub/sonny-davis/37/358/20b

> Hilary and Sonny are special people in my life. Sonny is one of my inspirations in putting this book project together. Thank YOU, Hilary and Sonny, for your contribution to this book project.
>
> ~ **Aime Hutton**

CHAPTER 22

MY SON, MY HERO

By Hilary Davis

Allow me to introduce you to my son, Sonny, and tell you why he is my inspiration and hero.

Sleep had totally evaded me. My heart pounded heavily as I lay waiting anxiously for the hours to slowly tick by. Finally, it was 5:30 a.m., time to go the hospital for the C-section.

Sonny was born on Friday, May 30, 1980, at precisely 8:38 a.m. and weighed in at 8lbs. 6ozs. All the preliminary tests taken at birth revealed nothing abnormal. He was a beautiful, blond-haired, blue-eyed, chubby, healthy, happy baby.

Sonny's toddler years revealed nothing abnormal either. He was active and displayed rather strong upper body strength and athletic abilities.

Then I started to notice something. Though Sonny ran around and was certainly able to keep up with everyone, he would trip a lot. He would pick himself up just as quickly as he went down, but I knew it was time to see a doctor. I was told that he was a child who just tripped over things. However, it kept happening, and so we trundled off to another doctor where I was told Sonny was being lazy about lifting his feet.

It's funny how a doctor's words can reassure you. I actually got used to Sonny tripping and believed everything was normal.

Just before Sonny's fifth birthday, we moved. At a visit to our new doctor, I said I didn't believe that there was anything wrong with him. I needed yet another opinion. The doctor chatted with Sonny, had him walk and run a bit, did a few reflex tests, and then said he wanted us to see a bone specialist.

In my ignorance, I thought we would see the bone specialist, who would have the answer to stop him from tripping. The specialist confirmed there was something wrong and referred us to a neurologist. That's when I began to worry. I took Sonny to the neurologist, who ordered a biopsy Sonny didn't even cry. He was such a trooper.

I will never forget the day we got the results of that biopsy. The nurse informed me the results were in but that we had to wait until after Christmas for the doctor to give us the full report. But I pressured her to give me the results. She reluctantly told me Sonny's test showed he had a form of muscular dystrophy (MD) called Charcot-Marie-Tooth disease (CMT). All I heard was muscular dystrophy then nothing else registered. I knew this was really serious. People died from MD. I was shattered. That Christmas was the most emotionally challenged holiday I've ever had. My sweet, active, happy baby boy had just been dealt a card I didn't know how to play. I couldn't fix it and make it right. Then denial set in. Sonny was more active than most children his age. They *had* to be wrong.

Finally, we got to see the neurologist again. He explained that CMT fell under the MD umbrella, along with forty other neuromuscular diseases. Luckily, CMT does NOT affect a person's lifespan. But Sonny somehow thought he heard the doctors say he wouldn't live past thirty years of age. I was shocked a few years ago when Sonny was speaking at a pep rally and I heard him tell a group of students this misinformation. I shudder to think how that must have impacted him all those years. Imagine living with that thought.

The peripheral nerves and muscles in Sonny's legs, feet, arms, and hands were affected. The degenerative nature of this condition causes these muscles to atrophy and waste away. Most who are diagnosed with CMT continue to walk, though with a peculiar gait. Some have such mild forms of the disease you would hardly notice it at all, while in others, the disease progresses into a more devastating condition. I prayed that Sonny had the less debilitating form. That, unfortunately, was not to be. Sonny is now thirty-four years old. He is unable to walk and uses a wheelchair daily. But even when he was younger, Sonny didn't let the disease stop him. Nor does it today.

Shortly before his thirtieth birthday, Sonny decided he needed to do something profound just in case his doctors were right. He swiftly organized a small humble pit crew and began rolling across Canada, starting at mile zero in the west. The campaign was to raise money, inspiration, and awareness for muscular dystrophy.

In Sonny's words:

"I have experienced many wonderful things in life, mostly due to the unconditional love I received from my mother, who, despite any physical limitations I may have had, was determined to get me involved in as many activities as possible. I had the opportunity to explore a variety of interests — wheelchair sports, competing in races, travelling with a marching band, participating in musical competitions, and being a sea scout. Unfortunately, due to my changing condition, my racing classification was pulled from me just as I began training for the 2008 Beijing Paralympics. With much bureaucracy and deliberation within the professional racing world, my Paralympic dream suddenly ended. But they couldn't take away my other dream. I was going to wheel across Canada in my hand-cycle.

I appreciate how lucky I was to have been exposed to some great individuals who inspired me tremendously to take on this challenge. I admire people like this as shining examples of personal freedom and power, people I consider to be my heroes — and by hero, I mean anyone that faces adversity with courage. I have been taught that having the courage to surrender and accept, to listen to and act upon our inner calling, to stand tall against our fears, and to love through and beyond our hurts is important. My heroes include my ever-supportive mother, the brave Terry Fox, and the unstoppable Rick Hansen."

My son drew from a well of inspiration over his thirty odd years and told me repeatedly he wanted to give back, to inspire others, and to honor his family, friends, and his heroes.

At thirteen years old, he received one of the highest scouting awards and the Governor General presented the medal to him. The mayor of Calgary presented him with a Great Citizen award, and the Optimist Association awarded him with a certificate. Recently, in Toronto, he received the Client of the Year award from the Muscular Dystrophy Association.

Sonny has always had big dreams. After a demanding start by conquering Canada's Rocky Mountains and the many fundraising stops along the way, "Sonny and Chair," as he is affectionately known, called journeys end in Thunder Bay, Ontario, after three months and nine days of pushing his hand-cycle on the shoulder of the TransCanada Highway. His dream was to go coast to coast but he was forced to recalibrate the end location with the sudden death of his father.

"I was satisfied with what I and my small humble team had accomplished and as we pulled into Thunder Bay, we made our way up to the Terry Fox memorial and finished with tears as we celebrated. Even after it was over, I still had the desire to inspire. My journey wasn't over yet."

Later in 2011, Sonny was asked to join Rick Hansen on his twenty-fifth anniversary cross-Canada relay. It involved seven thousand people—considered to be "difference-makers"—and they were all participating in the coast-to-coast relay. Sonny was chosen as one of the endurance athletes. He had been given another chance to fulfill his dream, only this time he would be travelling in the opposite direction, from the east coast to the west. Sonny got me involved too. I feel deeply humbled to have participated in such a historic event. I walked 250 meters, carrying the Rick Hansen Medal down an old country road on Prince Edward Island, with Sonny by my side. This was the last time my son was able to walk with me. His disease has progressed so much that he can only use his wheelchair now. But our spirits are not dampened, as we look forward to possible stem cell therapy to work a miracle for him.

I believe any disability is very difficult to live and cope with and I respect anyone who has a disability and manages to push through it and become successful.

Sonny likes to pose this question:

"What will it take to go beyond your limitations and live a wealthy, inspired life, to arrive on your death bed fully given, free of all doubt and regret, to

be content with this life, remembering contentment is wealth?" He say's I taught him how to do those things.

My son never ceases to amaze me. He has a "never give up" attitude. He is now working on producing a documentary film and an album, with all his own original music.

My son never ceases to teach me about life and to never give up!

Sonny is *my* hero.

Kheri Taylor-Milos, RSW

Kheri Taylor-Milos is a single mother of two extraordinary special needs children. She is a registered social worker, a passionate advocate for the disadvantaged, and a determined educator specializing in child abuse and mental health issues.

Kheri co-founded an organization, D&M Research Associates, in 2000 in order to provide professional development workshops regarding child abuse to agencies working with children. This branched into workshops presented at the Canadian Mental Health Association and local churches. Kheri herself has moved from surviving to thriving and will continue to encourage and empower others to do the same.

When I saw Kheri's photo, I knew she must be in this book! Her spirit and spunk is awesome. Thank YOU, Kheri, for being in this book project!

~ **Aime Hutton**

CHAPTER 23

NOT SURVIVING BUT THRIVING

By Kheri Taylor-Milos, RSW

Taneal was the fourth child out of six. Her father was the third trick of the night for her mom. At least, that's what she had been told. There were a string of "uncles" that drifted through her mother's life that had resulted with the younger twins. The family bounced from apartment to rundown house to low income housing on a regular basis—depending on finances. Or if Children's Services had become involved again. "Nosy b*****s," as her mom called them. Taneal had lived with three sets of foster parents by the time she was five. She gave up on having a stable home by the time she was seven. Her oldest brother was in a group home for kids with behavioral difficulties. Her oldest sister was in one foster home while the next sister was in a different group home. Their files were all "before the courts" while the director asked for a "permanent guardianship order." Taneal didn't understand any of it, other than that she and the twins were stuck with their mom while the others were free and not coming back.

Taneal supposed that her mother loved them "as best she could" (according to the ladies that were meeting with her mom every week), but Taneal's opinion was that her mom loved a bottle a lot more than her kids. Her mom pretended to listen to the workers, smiling and nodding and parroting the words, but then called them dirty names and told Taneal that she wasn't "going to do nothin' they said 'cause she'd raised children already and just because the government took them away didn't mean she had done a bad job; it was just a misunderstanding." Taneal thought the misunderstanding was that people kept giving her mom chances. Her mom finally ran out of chances when Taneal was nine, and she was placed in a foster home with her younger brothers, who were a very cute five.

Taneal didn't get to see her older siblings; there just wasn't a way to arrange people to drive and supervise a visit between all of them. Besides, she didn't really know them. And despite being angry with her mom, she missed her. Taneal hated her new school and started hanging out with the other kids who hated school. That led to her skipping classes and getting in trouble for being defiant with the teachers. Then she would get in trouble at "home," which led to her acting out, which led to the foster family telling the workers that they couldn't handle Taneal's attitudes and behaviors. Taneal was placed in another foster home specializing in children with intensive behaviors. She couldn't understand why no one was bothering to talk to her about WHY she was breaking her brothers' toys or yelling swear words at teachers or tearing up her foster sister's homework or cutting up her brand new dress with the kitchen scissors. Taneal refused to say goodbye to her brothers; they got to stay!

Taneal supposed this new foster home was OK, if you liked overly cheery, affectionate people. She grudgingly admitted to herself that having her own room that she could decorate herself was neat. But she was way too cool and cautious to say it out loud. Taneal just shrugged a shoulder when Sharon (you don't have to call me *mom*, you already have a mom) asked her if she liked it. There was a younger foster boy that lived there already and Sharon and Pete had a sixteen-year-old daughter of their own. Taneal was secretly excited to have an older "sister" but played it like she was bored with other kids. And damned if she would admit that she found that bouncy, excited, huggy little guy cute!

The next couple of years were really tough on everyone. Taneal couldn't seem to stop herself from getting angry and striking out. She stole from Heidi, ruined Heidi's things, and told numerous lies to get Heidi into trouble. All Heidi did was look at Taneal with sad eyes and said, "I forgive you." Which made Taneal even angrier. She didn't really want or mean to hurt Brian; it just sorta happened. He would pester her for hugs and to play until she finally would push at him or yell at him or call him names. Brian would end up crying, Sharon and Pete would end up talking to her about how it was "OK to be angry but not OK to hurt people because you're angry," and Taneal would end up grounded, wondering why she kept doing these things.

143

Sharon or Pete would ask Taneal to complete her chores or finish her homework and Taneal would just blow up. She would scream, swear, throw things, and (only once!) hit Pete—just hauled off and slugged him in the arm. They always talked to her gently and hugged her once she had calmed down from the emotions. But Taneal had heard Sharon crying in the night on a few occasions and Pete reminding her that they had known Taneal would be a difficult child to break through to. Apparently, she had something called RAD—whatever that meant.

Taneal didn't know when the shift happened. All she knew was that she slowly stopped hoping for a hug from Sharon and started going over to lean against her, knowing that Sharon would turn and wrap her in consistently soft, warm arms. She began volunteering to play with Brian and asking before just using Heidi's clothes. And she started finding reasons to help Pete work in the backyard garden. Taneal noticed that she was actually beginning to believe they might keep her instead of give up on her. And she was slowing down her desperate quest to have the rejection happen on her terms instead of being slapped with it unexpectedly. Taneal stopped skipping her therapy appointments and opened up with the counselor. The woman explained that all the things that Taneal had been doing over the years were symptoms of being bounced from home to home and never having a stable adult to show Taneal she was loved. The therapist told Taneal that the behaviors were an attempt at protecting herself from more loss and pain. She went on to state that Sharon and Pete had gone to many workshops and their own counseling sessions to understand what Reactive Attachment Disorder was and how to best support Taneal while she adjusted to living in a safe and secure home.

Taneal couldn't stop the tears that, at first, leaked out of her eyes and trickled down her cheeks. The dam completely broke when she walked out of the office and into the waiting room to see Pete and Sharon waiting for her, smiles on their faces. Taneal was not one of those girls who were pretty when they cried—tears poured out, snot dripped down, and her face turned red and blotchy. Sharon jumped up in concern, but Taneal shook her head and grabbed her in a tight hug. Pete joined in, gathering both ladies into his arms. They stood there, crying together for a while, before Taneal asked if a family meeting could be arranged that night.

Later that night, Taneal sat nervously on a chair facing her family. She hesitantly opened her mouth and found she had to clear her throat. "I just wanted to tell you all how sorry I am for everything I put you through and," a hiccup-sob escaped, "thank you for not giving up on me." Everyone (except for Brian, that is) dissolved into tears and hugs and laughter, sharing memories of some of Taneal's more interesting stunts.

This is a compilation of several children that I have worked with throughout my career as a social worker. It is, unfortunately, a very simplified recounting and a happy ending was not often a part of their lives. That being said, foster parents are vital and there are not enough who actually educate themselves sufficiently to understand the underlying reasons behind a child's behaviors and that there is hope for change. "Pete" and "Sharon" were heroes in sticking things out and that is what makes the essential difference in a child being able to make the journey from surviving to thriving. "Taneal" didn't wake up one day and suddenly things were OK; she saw the consistency of the adults in her life and that provided the safety she needed to let go of unhealthy coping skills. "Taneal" is now an adult with three children of her own. She has a fulltime job as a legal assistant, a loving partner, and a wonderful relationship with her "forever" family.

Inch by Inch

Laurie Crookell

Laurie is an international best-selling author, writer, speaker, and empowerment consultant. She holds a BA in economics, works as a math and literacy specialist for children with learning differences, and owns a freelance writing company, Where Words Are Art. Laurie's writing has been recognized in several writing competitions. Her essay, "Learning, Upside Down," won the 2010 Human Potential Nonfiction Writing Contest. Her picture books, *Aaron's Salmon* and *Frieda's Frogs*, have been finalists in the Writers' Union of Canada Writing for Children Competition. Two more children's stories, "Saving the Seahorses" and "Jennifer's Got Pizzazz," were recently short-listed in the 2013 Surrey International Writers' Conference Writing Contest.

You can connect with Laurie through:

www.lauriecrookell.com

✉ **lauriecrookell@shaw.ca**

f **facebook.com/laurie.crookell**

in **linkedin.com/pub/laurie-crookell/52/37/859**

> Laurie and I met on another book anthology project. We connected immediately and I knew she had to be a part of this book! Thank YOU, Laurie, for your support and brilliance!
>
> ~ **Aime Hutton**

CHAPTER 24

FINDING GRATITUDE THROUGH TRAUMA

By Laurie Crookell

I sat in the intensive care unit, arguing with truth's reality. Hushed whispers. Distressed moans. Anguished cries. The steady whine of life support. All pierced through antiseptic walls, attacking my outer calm, depleting me of hope.

I gazed upon my husband's body. A plastic tube protruded from his mouth, like some alien spacesuit from a fictional sci-fi movie. Except this wasn't a movie. This was real. This was my husband. His injuries were extensive, a prognosis grimmer than any I could have imagined.

Brain injury. The words spewed from the neurosurgeon's mouth like the ragged edges of broken glass. "Your husband has been in an accident. He has a severe brain injury." Exactly what that meant, no one knew. Would he live? Would he remain comatose? How long would his coma last? If he awoke, what then? No answers. No predictions. No time lines. No guesses. "We can only wait and see." Words rattling in an endless loop through my mind. *Wait and see. Wait and see. Wait and see.* Limbo. No man's land. Nothingness.

Heart's fear pulsed through my veins, rendering me desolate of strength's courage. I knew nothing about brain injury. Only the pitying stares of medical staff spoke of the suffering I would bear. Wild thoughts attacked me, emotions threatening to lacerate my heart, crushing it in a single blow.

My daughters. Angelic. Innocent. Aged two and four. What would the impact be on them? My heart crumpled, the agonizing wrench of a mother's dream vanished in the debris of a morning car accident. This wasn't the life I wanted for them. I dreamed of childhood's carefree days—climbing trees, exploring imaginative worlds, playful fun highlighting their days. I wanted to give them everything. Joy. Love. Security. Opportunity. The jagged edge of sorrow plunged. My heart exploded.

My children were born in trauma. A raging blizzard set winter's scene for my first child's birth. Critical complications during both pregnancies jeopardized my health and life. My deliveries weren't much better.

Yet two beautiful girls later, I had my perfect family. Life was bliss. Career. Home. Family. It was all mapped out, until tragedy catapulted us into another dimension; and, in one mighty blow, stole our dreams. September 28, 1998, life went on hold.

For three weeks, his coma enslaved him. Cheers greeted his emergence. I, alone, did not celebrate. His memory was gone—his memory of me, his children, himself. He emerged a child. His mind so delusional he needed to plot his escape; while dodging flaming arrows, flying samurai swords, machine guns, and grenades. Imaginary perils that only existed in spy novels—and in my husband's mind.

With warrior strength, I greeted each day, a strength withered by nightfall. He over-stimulated, screaming in agony when I merely breathed. His brain grew dark with violent thoughts and actions. Building. Rising, until one day, they erupted. Six men held him down, straight-jacketed him, sedated him, tied him to the bed. His thrashing screams reverberated through my heart, an indelible memory of the deepest pain, until his violence turned to me. I escaped, but I had seen his eyes. The manic desire to harm. This was brain injury.

Six weeks passed before my children could visit. My oldest hid in her closet. But my youngest agreed, her dimpled two-year old hand clinging to mine. We sat on bedside's edge, her innocent body curled in my lap. He stared at her, blankly, like she was a piece of furniture. No recognition, no memory, nothing.

My daughter said, "Hello," and watched him for a few minutes. She turned to me, soulful brown eyes glinting with tears, an intelligence and wisdom far beyond her years conveyed in the golden shimmers of her eyes. In her sweet, melodic voice that could make angels weep with its magical lilt, she whispered, "Mommy. That isn't my daddy."

Christmas marked his first visit home. Morning dawned with the blinding whiteout of a blizzard, snowflakes the size of mini marshmallows. He had no memory of "home" and didn't want to come. So he screamed, nonstop, the entire two-hour journey home in a raging snowstorm. I drove 25 km/hour (15.5 mph). Yet to him, we were in a James Bond movie, racing at top speeds, dodging bullets disguised as snowflakes. "Mom?" my four-year old asked, grief's pain etched in mystic blue eyes. "He isn't dad anymore, is he?"

Soon, he was home fulltime. His needs extensive, as he learned how to walk again and struggled to regain his speech and other faculties. With each gain he made, I discovered more damage. Though his progress astonished, his personality remained forever changed.

I watched, powerless as my children withdrew, acted out, their once-confident selves slipping away with each day. My youngest never smiled. Trauma merged into their play. Games with dolls and stuffed animals involved a character being injured. The story was the same. This guy's been hit by a car, now he's in a coma and only has half a brain. This was their world.

After six and a half years, burnout led to the end of my marriage. Reserving what little energy I had left, I chose to give it to my children. But my choice came at a heavy price. Legal battles, money issues, angry outbursts from those who disapproved.

Despair lingered on our doorstep, looking for cracks to seep into our souls. During our darkest months, I feared despair would win. Our house was in receivership. No heat. No car. Thirteen dollars to my name. My mother was dying of cancer in another province. My roof leaked every rainfall, through holes so large, roof rats with two-foot long tails came inside to play. Overwhelmed, burned-out, and in need of something to lift our spirits, an idea popped into my mind.

I gathered my daughters. We curled up in my bed; one girl snuggled on either side. At the top of the page, I wrote: "Gratitude List." I didn't expect to find much. Not so. We filled five pages. Effortlessly. That was the day I chose to cease my worry and change my thinking.

Yes, my children's trauma was real. But looking deeper, I discovered something else. I noticed their depth of character, their compassion and empathy. A rare intelligence cultivated within them. Gifts in art and writing emerged due to their enhanced understanding and ability to emote. I witnessed strength and courage, wisdom and maturity. Other children looked to them for advice and support. The seeds of leadership were born.

To quote C.S. Lewis, "Hardships often prepare ordinary people, for an extraordinary destiny."

For whatever reason, my daughters needed these experiences as preparation for their futures. I was raising leaders. Adversity was the foundational growth upon which their leadership would grow. Who was I to take that away from them? My job lay in teaching them how to rise to it. As my attitude shifted, so did theirs.

Slowly, life improved. But post-traumatic stress, with its insidious grasp, still plagued us. That's when Blizzard came into our lives—our Husky. Starving and abused, we adopted him into our home. Full of energy, mischief, and the most lovable heart I've ever known, he taught us how to laugh again. He inspired us to live in the moment. He brought us joy, pleasure, and unconditional love. Some say we healed him. I say he healed us.

Some Strategies for Finding Gratitude:

1. Take care of you. Burnout is very difficult to recover from, a lesson I learned the hard way. Maintaining our own energy and positive outlook paves the way for our children to follow. Plus, the happier and healthier we are, the greater our ability to listen and support our children.

2. Provide absolute unconditional love. Be generous with affection and warmth. Clear behavioral expectations are part of that, but loving our children through their moments of overwhelm provides immeasurable support.

3. Remind them how they've successfully handled past difficulties, complimenting them when they show strength and resiliency

4. Encourage a long-term perspective with the reminder that there will be happier days in their future.

5. Give children opportunities to create, as this provides an outlet for emotional self-expression.

6. Bring the joy of pets into their lives. Their affection and power of unconditional love will heal.

7. Write a gratitude list, and place it in a visible location, adding to it whenever someone feels inspired.

8. Teach children to help others so they see they are not alone.

9. Create a memory book of accomplishments, special cards, letters, messages, compliments, pictures of family and friends as a reminder of the positive things when they are feeling discouraged.

10. Create family memories. Celebrate birthdays and holidays. Spend time relaxing together, going for hikes and bike rides. Enjoying life feeds our souls so we don't deplete our energy by dealing only with the negatives.

Gratitude is born when we shift our thinking. Adversity builds the foundation of greatness, providing our children with strength and resiliency, enabling them to rise to their full potential. Embrace this gift.

Bonita Lehmann

Bonita Lehmann, an inspirational speaker and author of her own memoir, shares her story of the near-death of her daughter Samantha at eighteen months of age before she was finally diagnosed with Type 1 diabetes. Bonita shares a mother's journey—caring for a child with Type 1 diabetes, finger pokes to test blood sugars, and insulin injections that broke Bonita's heart into pieces every day. She went into survival mode to deal with the strict routine of a toddler with insulin dependent diabetes. Bonita learned many coping strategies and she supports others dealing with chronic illness.

www.dreambig-liveamazing.com

facebook.com/bonita.lehmann162

facebook.com/Dream-Big-Live-Amazing/329835009433

twitter.com/Bonita_Lehmann

linkedin.com/pub/bonita-lehmann/43/a3a/960

Bonita and I met through eWomen Network. Her drive to empower others is what drew me to ask her to be in the book. Thank YOU, Bonita, for being in this book with us!

~ Aime Hutton

CHAPTER 25

SAVING HER. SAVING ME.

By Bonita Lehmann

"Not my little girl!" I cried. "Not my sweet, little Samantha." October 1, 1994, was when my firstborn child, just eighteen months old, almost died before she was finally diagnosed with Type 1 diabetes, unusual for such a young child. On that horrific day, it was like my little baby was suddenly replaced—from a child that didn't have a care in the world to one that will have a life of needles, finger pokes, and a tight schedule of meals, snacks, and activity. The idea of watching my daughter grow up with careless abandon, dancing and being a free spirit had spoiled in the sun, shriveled up and blown away with the wind.

Type 1 diabetes, or insulin dependent diabetes, is an autoimmune disorder that destroys the insulin-producing cells in the pancreas. Samantha has a chronic illness that she will never grow out of and she will need insulin forever. Over the years, I constantly worried about Samantha. First there was the diabetes itself. The concern about low blood sugars, high blood sugars, her eating schedule, and when she started school was a whole new set of worry. Then she was dealing with her own blood testing at school and monitoring herself. How would she be able to grow up "normally" and fit in? And how could I help her "just be a kid?" I wondered.

At the hospital, there was a special clinic for kids with diabetes with specialists, dieticians, and family therapists that were wonderful, but I did my own research as well. I wanted to learn how to help her cope with the emotions that she might be experiencing. Having a chronic illness creates immense emotional stress and other reactions like fear of resentment and rejection, possible low self-esteem, and seeing the illness as a punishment. The incidence of depression is three times greater in a child with a chronic illness. Then, of course, there was the effect on the family itself. Diabetes had its cruel hold on all of us.

The years were difficult, with many emergency room visits, along with personal and family stress. However, today, at twenty-one, Samantha is a beautiful, happy, and successful university student going into her fourth year. She is a very intelligent and determined young woman that would make any mother proud. Diabetes has affected her life tremendously by making her less adventurous than most and always mindful about her actions. Diabetes also shaped her character as well, mostly by creating a deeper understanding for others, especially in times of struggle or distress. Her capacity for empathy is huge. She often sees the other side, because she has been there. She was ridiculed and bullied at school, and she has been ostracized on many occasions. She has also experienced constant physical and emotional pain for many years. This left a deep scar for poor Samantha, thus her empathetic nature that is unusual for a young person, but it is her most endearing quality. She is a beautiful creature on the inside, as well as the outside.

Being the mother of a child with a chronic illness deeply affected me, as well. There have been many lessons learned and mistakes made over the years. Today, however, I am proud of how I handled many challenges. One of the best situations I handled was when giving Samantha her insulin injections. I learned to slow down and make it more about her. Her daily injections were the most painful thing to do in my life and my heart broke into a thousand little pieces each time—and if my heart was breaking, what was happening to hers, I wondered. She was too young to say the words and explain, but I could see the pain in her eyes—her big beautiful brown eyes.

She needed injections twice a day, and sometimes even three times when she was sick. Sammy would cry, scream, and plead.

"No momma, no today. Peese."

Her tiny little voice, pleading as I was holding her down to give her the insulin injection, but I had no choice. I had no choice but to hurt my little girl every single day.

One morning, I just couldn't do it anymore. I couldn't keep holding her down. I needed to change the process. So, instead of me being frantic and Samantha being fearful about her injection, I slowed it down, shifted the energy, and made it more about her. I gave her back the control of her injections and created a more positive experience. As positive as it could be. Of course, it was still painful. It was a needle, after all.

In the new slowed down way, we would start by just taking a moment together. I would hold her on my lap, be still for a minute, and I would tell her that together we would "center." We would close our eyes, breathe deeply, and step out of the world and into a calm place. Then I would ask her if she was ready. By asking her and by waiting for her to tell me when she was ready, it was giving her control of what was happening. Instead of me controlling her, she was controlling her situation. It was empowering for her and transformational for everyone. This "centering," this kind of meditation, would take a bit more patience and a bit more planning, but the impact on our lives was monumental. The cool thing that also happened was as Samantha got older, she used this "centering" practice not just for injections but also for other stressful times in her life. This has become a life skill for her.

When she turned fourteen, she got an insulin pump and that changed her routine for the better. She no longer needed daily injections, as the pump would slowly infuse insulin all day long. She only needed to change her injection site once every three days and the danger of high and low blood sugars were greatly reduced. The pump was a godsend for both Samantha and the family.

The other big lesson learned was one that I didn't realize until much later. We created a support system for Samantha but I forgot about mine. I was so busy saving her, I forgot about saving me. I fell off my own priority list and forgot about the help that I needed. Over the years, I carried the burden alone and by doing so, I lost who I was and lost the belief in myself. Instead of letting others help and support me, I pushed them away and tried to do it all alone. I created a "one-mother" army instead. It was not a healthy environment for me. When Samantha switched to the insulin pump and I finally got a break in the routine, I took the time and turned it around for myself. Realizing that I had forgotten about me, I reached out to family and friends again and started to take better care of myself. One can only go so far alone and then you need to realize that you need help.

Slowly, I got back into a healthy routine of exercise and eating properly. I rediscovered my passion for the outdoors and embraced challenges previously I shied away from due to sheer exhaustion in dealing with diabetes and juggling a young family. It didn't take long before I was feeling energetic and alive; the best result was the weight I lost. I had been carrying it for many years. I became a happier, healthier me. Family, community, and support is how Samantha got through the tough times, and had I done the same, my struggles would have been easier and seemed less of a burden.

Looking back, hindsight is, of course, 20/20. The advice I would offer to others dealing with chronic illness or a challenging family situation is not to forget about your own support system. Don't forget to save yourself while saving everyone else. Be a top priority on your own list, and you can be more effective as a mother or caregiver—wise words but sometimes difficult to follow when you're being pulled into the messiness and daily minutiae of a chronic illness. It is very important to keep reminding yourself. It is a daily task, this self-reminder. Each day brings uncertainly, the stress of that on its own needs the best possible *you*, every day.

Is your energy optimal to support those who rely on you? Do you have or are you building your own supportive community? Being ready for what the day may bring means to be well-rested with proper nutrition and have a supportive network around you. This is how we are at our best for our children and in turn, have the patience to make the challenging days less challenging, to slow down and shift the energy of those challenging days instead of being frantic and stressed. Who are you saving today?

Val Neighbors

Award-winning Val Neighbors, home care sales consultant, speaker and TV personality, loves all things sales related. Val successfully built a 1.1 million-dollar business in just over twenty-four months from the ground up, putting her in the 1.8 percent group of women-owned businesses to achieve the million-dollar annual revenue mark. Her sales strategies help other health care businesses achieve the same level of growth and profitability she accomplished for herself.

Upon meeting Val for the first time, you'll immediately be drawn into her passion for life. Val's network is not only wide but deep through connections with her clients, business associates, and friends.

www.valneighbors.com

f **facebook.com/val.neighbors**

⊙ **twitter.com/valneighbors**

in **linkedin.com/in/valneighbors**

Val and I are Facebook friends. She wanted to be in this book to share her story with you. Thank YOU, Val, for your support and energy for this project. I appreciate YOU!

~Aime Hutton

CHAPTER 26

LIFE IS A JOURNEY, EMBRACE EACH STEP
By Val Neighbors

I knew for quite some time that something was "off" with me and chalked it up to the amount of times I moved as a kid. I attended six different schools from kindergarten to my senior year in high school. Oh, how I blamed my parents for so long for torturing me. I was always the new kid looking in from the outside. I was naturally a shy little girl but found myself being forced to talk to people if I ever stood the chance of being accepted. As if being new wasn't bad enough, I was also the tallest girl or second tallest girl in my class. Ugh, why did I have to be gargantuan? I heard things like "Amazon girl," "How's the weather up there?" "Man, you're tall," and "You're gigantic." Whoa, talk about bruising the confidence of an already fragile girl. How can kids be so inconsiderate? Back in that day, we didn't use the term *bully* but as I'm sure you can tell it definitely was a form of bullying.

High school led to some tough and deep challenges. I started my freshman year in an all-girls Catholic high school in Pennsylvania, which actually wasn't so bad. We didn't have the boys to impress, so I literally rolled out of bed, washed my face, brushed my teeth, threw my hair up, put my uniform on, and out the door I went. My father was transferred the summer between my freshman and sophomore year so we move to New Jersey prior to me starting school. Oh no, not again! Just when I thought I had established some friendships that would take me through some of the most challenging years, I once again found myself starting over, trying to develop new friendships. New Jersey brought on some new surroundings and opportunities. I was lucky enough to end up in public school due to my mom not knowing the area and location of Catholic schools. YIPPEE, I finally got to wear "real" clothes after being in a uniform since kindergarten!

Little did I know, real clothes brought judgment. My dad worked for JC Penney, so we shopped there for our clothes since he was fortunate enough to receive a discount. Apparently, the "in" crowd shopped at stores like Benetton. Oh, how I loved those clothes! I often got picked on for the clothes I selected and wore from JC Penney. During the last three years of high school, I tried my best to "float" around and not be tied to one particular group. Although I thought I was pretty successful, I found myself being called out for fights. Why did other girls want to fight me? Was it the fact that I was tall? Was it because I wasn't afraid to speak my mind? Was it because I was a pretty girl (once finally I made it through the awkward, pimple phase)? Whatever the reason, I once again endured being bullied. It wasn't cool but it happened.

My senior year was a pretty rough one. I almost didn't graduate because I decided I no longer wanted to live under my parents' roof with rules. I moved out and in with my boyfriend, who had already graduated high school. Yep, not exactly one of my smartest decisions but it was a decision. Looking back, I don't remember exactly how long I was out of my parents' house, but I don't recall it being longer than a couple of months. Due to my not attending school for a couple of months, I ended up having to make up the time. I didn't get to walk with my graduating class but did receive my high school diploma. Right about now, most people figured I'd end up working a low paying job and not amounting to anything in life.

After high school, I continued trying to find myself. I decided not to attend college and worked several different jobs, one of which laid the foundation for my future—but I didn't know it at the time. I took a job as a certified nurse's aide working in a nursing home. I'll never forget the smells, the mistreatment, the lack of family coming to visit, or the sheer fact that our aging adults were thrown into an institution and left to die. I believe this was the beginning of my awakening. I didn't last longer than a year in that job before moving into a new field. I decided that law enforcement was my calling, so I started school and worked part-time as a receptionist for a computer distributor. One evening changed the rest of my life…for the better.

The VP of sales came to me one night to let me know that several compliments had been made regarding my ability to handle the customers, staff, and vendors with professionalism and "out of the box" customer service. He offered me a job as an inside sales person. Ha, ha, ha, I laughed. I told him that I was NOT a used car salesman or a door-to-door salesman and wasn't interested. He gently reminded me that I was talking to the VP of sales! Oops, I thought! I apologized, and he ended up convincing me to give it a whirl. The next week my new journey began. I LOVED SALES! I loved every aspect of being in that position—connecting with people, learning about their personalities, asking questions, finding solutions, delivering amazing products, and creating raving fans. It was exhilarating to say the least. I ended up being recruited by one of my customers and then recruited by one of their customers, which led me to a large corporation, and I relocated to Northern New Jersey. Then the next big wall came crashing down. The woman who hired me left shortly after my arrival and the Wicked Witch of the West appeared as my new boss. I went from waking up, kicking my heels to go to work, to dreading Monday morning until Friday afternoon. I was eventually "laid off"—to this day I believe that was nonsense. I was in Northern New Jersey by myself with no job. After a temporary and yucky job working in New York City, which by the way was my first experience in the Big Apple, I ended up coming back to Southern New Jersey. (You'll have to wait for my own book to come out before you hear the rest of the story about NYC.)

I started working with a few headhunters, and BAM, one of the most amazing opportunities arrived. I was hired by a tiny company called Panasonic. I was one of their sales associates, traveling up and down the East Coast. I worked for them, and then Xerox, before leaving the workforce briefly to have my oldest son. I entered the world of sales just four short months after my son was born. I was a sales and marketing representative for a couple of hospices until my prior accountant talked me into opening my own business. WHAT? Was he crazy? I knew how to sell but I knew nothing about operations and HR. But it was by far the best decision I ever made. I generated six figures in eight months and 1.1 million dollars in just over twenty-four months of being in business. I am honored and proud of this achievement, especially since I almost didn't graduate high school and I don't have a college degree. To make it all a bit sweeter, I sold the business after six and a half years in October of 2013, after only two months of having it for sale.

The greatest lesson in all of it is that if it weren't for me being the outsider and having to "fight" my way to be part of the groups, and having the tenacity to keep going after what I wanted, I would have never built a successful company. You can't let anyone hold you back or hold you down—and that includes yourself. If you think it and dream it, you can achieve it. There is no time for me to judge those who wronged me along the way. I only have time to embrace them with love and forgiveness and hope that someday, they too find themselves and their way.

Inch by Inch

Richelle Traversano

Richelle Traversano is an author and motorcycle enthusiast. She is currently working on her second book. Richelle is a firm believer that chocolate and laughter will see you through the tough times. Never one to shy away from adventure and self-improvement, she has recently lost over one hundred pounds. She is learning to navigate through the world since the loss of her mother, and she will hug you tighter and longer than sometimes necessary. Richelle is a proud Canadian but prefers American pricing.

Follow her blog at

www.richellewrites.com

Reach Richelle at

 richelleauthoress@gmail.com

Richelle's story of courage and tenacity is amazing. I am honored and grateful to have you be a part of our book. I hear it's a dream come true for you to write in this book!

~ Aime Hutton

165

CHAPTER 27

SCAR TISSUE

By Richelle Traversano

When I was fourteen years old, I had a non-malignant cyst removed from my tailbone. This was/is a common surgery, however the physical and emotional scar it left behind was not.

Because of its location on my lower back, it was always covered up by clothing. The surgeon said it would heal in time and barely be noticeable. I had just turned fourteen and I was a happy kid. I loved to read and was cognizant of world issues. I understood that many children all over the world experience unthinkable pain and suffering and unfavorable circumstances, so I wasn't about to let a scar be my undoing. No one but me could see it, so, no big deal right?

Well, it never healed properly. I hadn't realized that. I had much more important issues at hand. Fourteen-year-old girl issues. If you're female, you understand. If you're male, you may have witnessed it.

So one day I decided to go swimming.

It was a fun day with my best friend. We swam, we laughed, we snacked, and we swam some more. The pool was getting ready to close so it was time to call it a day.

Cue the locker/change room.

I was standing at my locker, wrapped in my towel, digging through my backpack for my clothes. A two dollar bill fell out, so I knelt down to pick it up.

My towel dropped.

Behind me were a group of three girls. They noticed my back. I felt them notice it. Up until this point, my mom and doctors were the only people who had seen it. For a moment I froze. I was completely naked physically, and in an instant, emotionally naked too. My thoughts were swift—maybe they won't think anything of it, maybe they have bad vision and can't see it, maybe they'll notice the two dollar bill lying on the floor and forget about my back, maybe they…NO.

Their words were mean. Very mean. With each name they called me, they brought that scar to life. They laughed and they pointed, and by the time they were done, the scar was no longer a dormant feature on my body. It became a hideous entity.

A simple scar that never healed properly. A scar that used to signify a positive marking because it meant it wasn't malignant. A scar that showed I could brave surgery at that age. Now a scar morphed into an invisible heavy weight that I would carry.

I went home. I was hurt. I was affected by their words.

Up until that day, I never really looked at the scar. Sure, I had taken glances in the mirror but I never REALLY LOOKED at it. But it was time to look. It was time to get to know it. Was it what nightmares were made of? Was my back Frankenstein's counterpart? I had to figure out how complete strangers could turn words into soul-piercing weapons at the sheer sight of it—a naive endeavor but I was only a kid. So I dropped my pants, aligned my body in the bathroom mirror, and took my first investigative look.

The next thing I remember was waking up in my mom's arms on the bathroom floor. I'd passed out and she'd heard the thud. She was always my superhero. And with her superhero powers, she was there to rescue me. I was crying. The vision of what I saw in the mirror, combined with the words those girls said, came rushing back to me. I would have been on the floor again if I wasn't there already. I looked up at my mom and saw the pain she was feeling for me in her eyes. It was a moment I won't forget. No one likes to see their parents sad, and vice versa with their children, so I gathered my composure, pulled up my pants, and dried my teary face.

An appointment was made to see the doctor. I wanted answers. I wanted to understand why it healed the way it did. I wanted it fixed. I no longer wanted to get to know it, but it was etched in my mind and I could still hear those girls laughing at me.

The appointment wasn't for a few more weeks. I was becoming increasingly bothered by the fact that I was letting the scar and those mean words invade my thoughts and my life. It was distracting me in all areas—from school and sports to friends and family. I became very self-conscious. I would panic in locker rooms and hide out in bathroom stalls to get changed. At sleepovers, I would make myself sick with worry until I was changed into my pajamas and no one witnessed the hideousness. And forget about wearing a bathing suit. I was trying to avoid another swimming pool incident where ever I went. I did not want to be called those names again.

But putting all this worry and effort into hiding from words and a scar was starting to brew feelings of guilt. It was festering until it bloomed into a giant ball of guilt and anger. "How dare I feel this way!" I would shout in my mind. The "there are people all over the world who survive challenges and atrocities every day, and you're bent over being called names?" thoughts would flood me.

It was a vicious, confusing circle.

Sitting in the plastic surgeon's waiting room, I felt so close to being done with scars and mean words. The finish line was in site and I was more than ready to cross it—sprint through it actually. But just as I was about to break the threshold banner and claim my participation ribbon, I noticed an open three-ring binder on the table.

Page after page of before and after surgery photos filled the binder. My eyes had never witnessed images of this nature. Women getting bigger breasts and stomach surgeries, and eye and face alterations, and if those didn't shake me up, the next ones did.

People with scars. Large ones. Medium ones. Small ones. Painful looking ones. Jagged ones. Straight ones. Lumpy ones. And bumpy ones. They were all in plain view on the pages and right there on their bodies.

Those scars were bad. Mine was just...different. My heart sank.

I had a moment of clarity for the first time since the swimming pool. I did not want the surgery. I would not go under the knife because of words. Not for a minute longer would I allow myself to be influenced by fear—fear of what others thought and fear of my own body and the scar that now came with it!

This was not the finish line. This was indeed the start.

Even though I declined the surgery, I was still curious about the scar's appearance. I was open to getting to know it again, since it was going to be a permanent fixture. I learned that when the cyst was removed, the surgeon used a procedure called a Z-Plasty to close the incision— aptly named for the appearance it leaves behind. The incision opened up at the top and bottom of the wound while I was still recovering in the hospital, but the doctor never repaired it, stating that it would heal itself. It didn't. Its shape and size grew due to scar tissue. And that's how the scar came to be.

Looking back, I am proud of the younger version of me who did not make a drastic decision based on hurt feelings and fear. Instead, I grew from this experience inch by inch and day by day. My family helped me through it every step of the way. Their love and support kept me strong. I wish my mom was still with us. I could sure use one of those superhero mom hugs after this walk down memory lane. I will make sure to give my dad an extra big one next time I see him.

I still have the scar. It could have been fixed at any time, but it's a reminder to me that scars should not define us. We are not our scars, we simply *have* them. It's oddly shaped and it's weird looking and a little fascinating too, but aren't all the things we love?

If there's a lesson to be learned from this little moment in time, it would be this—Words have power. Please use them for good. Always.

Annie Pool

Annie Pool lost her hair on her cancer vacation in November 2013, and was able to write this story about her daughter's hair loss from her own personal perspective. In 2014, the duo started Transform Travel, offering personalized shopping tours to locals and visitors in their home city of Victoria, BC. Their greatest passion and enjoyment is giving women with cancer an amazing VIP shopping experience that not only helps them see how beautiful they are but also helps them find clothes that will help them conquer their cancer.

I met Annie through eWomen Network. I love her never-give-up attitude for everything she does. Thank YOU, Annie, for being in this book with us!

~ Aime Hutton

CHAPTER 28

LETTING GO, HAIR BY HAIR
By Annie Pool

Have you ever been so frustrated you just wanted to tear your hair out?

What if you did and were unable to stop until you were nearly bald?

One day, my eleven-year-old daughter came home from school with two quarter-sized bald spots on her head. "What happened to your head, sweetie?" I asked the next morning, suppressing a gasp as I ran a comb through her tangled mess of blonde curls. "Oh nothing," Sarah said calmly. "My friend told me I should pull out my hair instead of chewing my fingernails."

Strange, I thought, but dismissed the phenomenon.

Nearly two years later, something that had begun so innocuously was now a serious problem. Sarah was merely a shadow of her former self. Her eyebrows were sparse, her eyelashes were missing, and there were noticeable bald spots on top of her head. Worse was the sad, empty look reflected in her eyes. How long until she was completely bald?

Desperate, I turned to the Internet. Searching Google for "hair pulling" produced a scientific term—trichotillomania, the compulsive urge to pull out one's hair. I learned this social disorder is an addictive behavior that leads to noticeable baldness, distress, and social or functional impairment.

I read about teens whose lives were ravaged by a condition that began in their childhood, persisting for decades—sometimes even for a lifetime. In the 1990s in the US alone, it was estimated that there were between 6–8 million sufferers of trichotillomania.

In horror, I tried to shrug off the shocking news—my daughter had a mental disorder. I spiraled into a deepening depression, wondering if her disorder had its roots in a story that began before she was even born.

That story began for me when I was seventeen and irresistibly drawn to the rebellious, anti-religious streak of my "soon-to-be" husband, hoping to escape my own oppressive church background. Six months after we married, he suddenly embraced religion in an extreme way, giving up all worldly ways and possessions, and spending endless hours with his spiritual guru—the leader of his own fledgling cult. Together the two of them strictly forbade me from any contact with friends or family.

Sarah was born a year later—a beautiful angel who came to visit me in the darkest hour of my life. While most newborns are welcomed into this world with a nursery lovingly decorated by their parents, Sarah had no such place prepared for her. "Home" for us was a communal lodge shared with four other people in the middle of nowhere in Kleena Kleene, BC.

Life now had taken on new hellish proportions. After a traumatic delivery, I had little time to recover from the effects of childbirth. Despite being severely anemic, I was cooking meals and cleaning the homes for all the other residents. Every day was strictly regulated, leaving me with little time to feed and care for Sarah. But when I could be with her, she was like an oasis of peace and tranquility in the middle of a cold, dark storm.

By late summer, the spiritual leader, his wife, and another woman left the group with the hope of starting a new one in the Netherlands. With nowhere to go, and nothing but a pickup truck and a fifteen-foot trailer, we connected with a similar community of believers who lived high up in the mountains in Idaho. For seven months, we lived with twenty-two people in a one-room house—no running water, no electricity, and very little food. Later that winter, Sarah became so severely dehydrated that her eyes rolled back in her head and her arms and legs flailed at her side. I, too, was very ill. Being so high up in the mountains meant there was no doctor available, but somehow, both of us miraculously recovered with the help of faith and a little rice, bananas, and tea.

Many times I wondered, "Had these early wounds scarred Sarah for life?" All I'd ever wanted was to provide a safe, loving home for her and her brother. I feared there might be a connection between these turbulent years and Sarah's hair pulling, but since her father strictly forbade her from receiving any counseling, my hands were tied.

Instead, I did what I could with the tools I had gleaned from the Internet. I tried everything to find a cure, from changing her diet to regulating her sleeping patterns, using behavioral modification techniques and keeping a journal to track the amount of times — as well as when and where — she pulled out her hair each day.

I wrote out inspiring Bible verses about faith and trust and believing in the impossible, and hung them from her bed posts. I prayed to God, surrendered to him, pleaded with Him, and yet…nothing. I was a nightmare to be around — constantly nagging, worrying, cajoling, and handwringing — driving a deep impenetrable wedge between the two of us.

My motto for life had always been "in acceptance lies peace." I believed good things came out of bad, so I thanked the heavens without ceasing until I felt like a crazy person, choking out words of gratitude too difficult for me to utter. And still nothing.

Then one day, a light broke through.

I had been reading *Prison to Praise*, a book explaining the importance of gratitude in all things, even things we don't like or understand. I came across a story that ignited fresh hope within about a prisoner in jail who learned to be grateful in the most unusual way. After reading *Prison to Praise*, he scoffed at its advice but then he took up the challenge to utter his own words of gratitude in an angry, spiteful way, scanning the sad saga of his life in search of horrible circumstances for which to be thankful. Finally, one day, his heart burst open with the most profound gratitude.

"Now that's something I can do!" I'd thought. If he could be a devil about it and find peace, maybe I could too.

That day, I found a big, fuzzy pile of blonde hair on the bathroom floor. I decided to throw my whole self into venting all the defiant, bitter, angry feelings that had been simmering below the surface for years. "Thanks a lot that Sarah's nearly bald," I moaned, "that she is taunted by her friends at school, that she has a debilitating disorder and will probably struggle with shame and guilt for the rest of her life! Thanks a whole bunch!"

"Thank you that I feel like I'm losing my mind, that I'm no longer the happy mother I used to be, and that I'm so frustrated and despairing, I feel like pulling out my hair! Thanks a whole lot!" It felt so good to express how anguished I felt. I continued this unusual form of gratitude for days, exhausting every negative circumstance I could conjure up in my mind.

One day, I felt like my soul had been set free. My whole heart had flooded with immense joy. I no longer cared if Sarah pulled out her hair, if she went completely bald, or even if she had this disorder for the rest of her life. It wasn't that I was indifferent or calloused. I was simply, wonderfully, and completely 100 percent OK with all of it — period. I was transformed.

Sometime later, Sarah tried to pull her hair out again, but this time, she was completely overcome with a violent urge to vomit.

That was the last time she pulled out her hair.

Gradually, her hair came back in — the most unusual blend of long and short hair. We were both deliriously happy to see the new growth. As her hair evened out, it was a beautiful sign that new growth takes place when all appears barren.

Today the bond between us is unbreakable. Sarah sees now how incredibly resilient she is. She is immensely proud of her hair.

One thing is for sure: struggles can make us heroic — no one becomes a hero by scaling molehills; heroes are made by scaling mountains. It is during adversity we learn our most valuable lessons, especially the beauty of trusting and letting go of control. We learn how wonderfully resourceful, self-reliant, courageous, and patient we can be. Most of all, we learn to persevere, to keep going no matter how dark the storm and no matter how wild the seas, because beyond the darkest night lies the brightest morning.

My deepest wish for Sarah is that through all her experiences, the good and the bad, she endlessly blooms into a beautiful flower too bright to behold.

Breya Hardy

Breya is a graduate of the University of Calgary Faculty of Medicine with her bachelor's in community rehabilitation and a certified A.D.A.P.T. dance instructor. Early in her career, she established herself as a respected choreographer and music director throughout Alberta and had the privilege of travelling the world as a performer. Although she has dedicated over a decade to her formal education, Breya's most invaluable lessons have come from her connection to Spirit and her precious son, Bowen. Breya is a professional psychic medium, certified Reiki Master, and Healing Touch for Animals practitioner, using her spiritual gifts for healing humans and animals alike.

www.brightlightworker.com

www.youngliving.org/breyabomba

www.livingtoseizetheday.blogspot.ca

f   **facebook.com/livingtoseizetheday**

Breya's story of her son is powerful, and I honor Breya for writing for this project even with her little one still not out of the woods. Brerya, thank YOU for being in this book project!

~ **Aime Hutton**

CHAPTER 29

THE ART OF BEING SPIRIT

By Breya Hardy

After eight miscarriages, four months of bed rest, fifty-five hours of labor, and an emergency C-section, our miracle boy arrived close to 11 p.m. on November 11, 2011. Bowen (Bo) was premature but healthier than a horse and stronger than an ox, as my Grandma would say. We instantly fell in love with the little miracle we had waited so long for.

During the first month of Bo's life, I continually told him to stay a baby. He was growing so quickly, I wanted to stop the clock and keep our little man teeny tiny. Then on December 17, 2011, the unthinkable happened.

Our new little family was driving home from Bo's first Santa visit. My husband, Devon, and I were singing Christmas carols when I looked over to admire our beautiful baby. My heart stopped as I realized his lips were dark blue and his eyes were bulging out of his head. He wasn't breathing. I yanked him from his car seat and his body was as limp as a ragdoll. I started screaming "BREATHE! BREATH!" while patting his back, trying to bring him back to life. He finally gasped for breath, and in the blink of an eye, we were standing in the PICU at the Alberta Children's Hospital.

"Are you the mother?" A doctor slid the curtain aside to reveal a line of people in white coats. Me? I was the mother. The mother of that baby fighting for his life.

The interrogation started: "Describe your medical history, pregnancy, and labor, and delivery." The brainstorming followed: "Maybe he was choking, maybe the baby's condition is a result of the mother's condition." Everyone had the best intentions but it didn't matter because no one had answers. Doctors finally concluded that Bo was born at thirty-six weeks, "a strange age when strange things happen." He was sent home on oxygen and they reassured us he would only need it for a few months. By spring, he would be a healthy baby.

They were wrong. Right after Christmas, Bo was hospitalized with pneumonia. A few weeks later, the seizures started. Our lives began to spiral out of control as we realized he wasn't getting better, he was getting worse. The Alberta Children's Hospital became our home as we searched for answers. Days were long, nights were longer, and we lived in a constant state of fear for our child's life. It was impossible to understand how something like this was happening to our family.

On September 3, 2012, Bo's neurologist diagnosed him with a rare form of epilepsy affecting his autonomic nervous system. He was sent home on seizure medication. Doctors were confident the seizures would eventually stop and Bo would develop into a typical child.

The next thirty days were hell. Bo's seizures tripled and he became extremely aggressive. We were losing him to a fog of pharmaceutical side effects. I cried every day. Some days, I just lay on the kitchen floor, sobbing and paralyzed. The previous nine months we had obsessed over getting a diagnosis and "fixing" our child. The day after Bo received his diagnosis, I just wanted to give it back.

October hit and we took Bo off his seizure medication, put him on a new one, and prayed. Within five days, Bo's seizures started to decrease and he started smiling again. Another three weeks passed and he began sitting by himself, rolling over, and even had an appetite for the first time. Our baby came to life overnight, thanks to new medication and a miracle.

As Bowen's first birthday approached, we were ready to celebrate! When everyone started singing happy birthday, I looked up at all the smiling faces and burst into tears. We had made it. Everyone says when you have a baby it goes so fast. I can honestly say that first year went so slow it felt like ten years. We wanted Bo to be bigger, older, and stronger so he could be safer. It felt so surreal to celebrate our miracle man that day.

Then November 12 happened. Bo spiked a fever of 104. Back to the hospital we went where he battled RSV for a month. Over the next seven months, Bo was constantly sick, and not typical colds and flus: measles, croup, pneumonia, a staph infection, rotavirus—I can't remember the rest. With every illness came more seizures. We had such a small window of what life was like with a healthy child, it was devastating to watch our child slip away from us again.

One particular night during the early spring, I was rocking Bo to sleep when he pointed to door and exclaimed, "Angels, mama!" A few weeks prior, he had started referring to our dogs as "the angels" so I assumed he was looking for them. Then he pointed towards the window and said it again. Bo was right. All through our hospital room tiny orbs of light were floating and a sense of peace had filled the air. It wasn't the dogs Bo was looking for, he was pointing at God's angels who had come to visit us.

This was my wakeup call. Throughout my entire life, I had seen, felt, heard, and even talked to all sorts of angels and spirits. When Bo became sick, I went into survival mode and lost all sense of my Higher Self. I somehow forgot that although we are human, we are Spirit first. As we watched the angel orbs, I shook my head as everything I had ever known came flooding back to me. I sat there in disbelief, realizing that while we had been nurturing Bo's body and mind that entire time, we hadn't thought to nurture his spirit and soul.

Immediately, we started using therapeutic quality essential oils, herbs, and other natural remedies that had somehow become a distant memory since Bo's birth. We stopped eating the cafeteria food and filled the hospital fridge with balanced organic meals. Bo started seeing a cranial sacral therapist, chiropractor, and one of the best acupuncturists and Chinese medicine doctors in Canada. Our lives transformed as energy healing and vibrational medicine became our second language. When we were out of the hospital, we made having fun and creating beautiful memories our first priority and when we were in the hospital, we figured out how to do the same. Not only was our entire family (furries included) getting physically healthy, but our hearts were healing too. In the spring of 2013, our entire family came to life. Unlike the first time, Bo stayed healthier and happier than we could have ever imagined. Our family grew stronger, as we finally understood what it meant to live in love and light.

It has been a year and a half since that night my Spirit was reawakened. It surprises me to say that it's only been a year and a half because those dark and fearful times feel like so long ago. That's not to say we don't still have our challenges. Recently, doctors found the source of Bo's ongoing medical mysteries: an autoinflammatory disease called Cyropyrin-Associated Periodic Syndrome (CAPS). We still have moments of unbearable anger, guilt, and sorrow but that's the difference between then and now. They are just moments. We are all human. We need to experience the true raw emotion of what it means to be human. Although the bad days still sting and the tears still flow, my faith continually holds strong. To live is to learn and to learn is to live the life your Soul has chosen—to the fullest.

I wish I could take away your pain, but I can't. No one can. But we can give you support, love, and gentle suggestions that have helped us along the way.

Take as much time as you need to be human. Once these moments start to quiet, you will have to make a choice: to agonize over tomorrow or to live for today. Some days, it will feel impossible, but that's OK. Be gentle with yourself and turn to the guidance of your Higher Self.

Drink water. Our physical bodies are 80 percent water, and every ounce of it carries a vibration. When we nourish our bodies, we strengthen our souls and raise our own vibration.

The most inspirational souls take the bodies of tiny children we call superheroes. They come straight from heaven with a mission to teach, learn, and inspire. They may appear weak and vulnerable but each has the Spirit of a lion. Don't underestimate them.

It is a blessing and a curse to feel all that encompasses mankind. Enlightenment can lead to the most incredibly divine gifts. Peace. Unconditional love. Forgiveness. Acceptance. It doesn't lessen the pain we feel, but it does brighten the light we live in. We are all human, but we can't forget that we are mostly Spirit, and the art of being Spirit is absolutely exquisite.

Marc J. Wagner

Marc J. Wagner was born in Bamberg, Germany, in June, 1974. In January, 2009, he moved to Florida.

Marc was always interested in spirituality and music, being that he grew up with a very intuitive and artistic grandmother.

Marc had quite a lot of health-related challenges during his childhood, starting with a very complicated surgery when he was only three months old. He will share one of his most profound healing stories with you in this book.

In his free time, Marc loves to play guitar, be in nature, and read books that help the soul evolve.

Marc and I met through mutual friends. He is an amazing man who has a powerful story to share with you. Thank YOU, Marc, for being in this book project!

~ **Aime Hutton**

CHAPTER 30

MOM—MY HERO AND GUARDIAN ANGEL

By Marc J. Wagner

My life started out just like anyone else's, I would say—I was born by my mother.

It was almost midnight on June 27, 1974, in Bamberg, Germany, the town where I was born and lived in for thirty-three years. It was a natural birth without complications, and after eight hours of labor, she was able to hold me in her arms for the first time.

I am the second child of two. I do have an older sister who is six years older.

My father was a young business man just stepping in to the footsteps of his father, who founded the family business in 1950 in Bamberg.

When my father joined the company, we had only one location, but through my father's enthusiasm and efforts, the company grew rather quickly to a nice medium-sized company with four locations by the time I was born. I do remember from early childhood that he was working most of the time, and when he was home he needed quiet time because he had a lot of stress and troubles at work and was often in a bad mood because of that. I always said that I grew up mostly without a father figure and the father figure I did experience was grumpy and rarely in a good mood. He always said he was doing this for us so we could have a financially worriless life. The problem is that as a child, you don't really worry about money. All you really want as a child is a dad who actually acknowledges you and plays with you every now and then.

So I was never really able to build a normal relationship with my father until later in life.

My mother was more of the soft and loving kind of personality, and there were times where I wished that she would leave him because I saw she was suffering under his mood swings.

Today, I am aware that he did the best he could with experiences he had in his childhood and throughout his life. And by understanding this, I was able to grant forgiveness and to find peace.

After I came home with my mother from the hospital, the odyssey began.

I remember my mother telling me that I dealt with a lot of infantile colic issues and therefore cried a lot, and often, very hard. She also had my sister to take care of.

And then one day, when I was just about three months old, I must have cried so much and so hard that I got a hernia in my right groin! So I had to have my first surgery when I was just three months old.

But it didn't end there. After approximately four weeks, I experienced the second hernia on the left groin. This time they had to put me in ICU for four weeks without anyone from my family allowed to see me, except through a window. I guess that's just how it was back then.

As I am writing about this now, I am actually experiencing a tightening in my chest and I feel the onset of an anxiety.

And then thinking about how my poor mother and other family members must have felt seeing their baby lying there in the hospital crib without being able to comfort or touch him.

Thank God, I survived. And there were times where it wasn't all that clear.

After that, I had a rather challenging childhood because of a messed up and weakened immune system due to all the medication I had to take so early in life.

My immune system was wrecked at a very early age and one illness led to another. Whenever something was going around in school or in the family, I was sure to get it sooner or later.

Then when I was eight years old, my tonsils had to be removed due to the chronic troubles I had every time cold or flu season came around.

After those were removed, I gained a lot of weight, which some kids at school found very funny and called me names.

That's when the bullying at school started. In the beginning, I just laughed it off and didn't think too much about it, but I told my mother what had happened and without me knowing, she took action. And first, she talked to the teachers I had at that time and asked them to keep an eye on the students who bullied. But that didn't help too much. So one day, my mother went into my classroom and talked to each of those kids herself, and the bullying stopped.

Besides the chronic bronchitis and sinusitis I had all my life, I also dealt with Neurodermatitis, which is a skin condition that leads to very annoying, constant itching and scratching of the skin usually in multiple places.

It was mainly on my hands, arms, and knees. After some very long and painful treatments, it finally subsided…but then I must have picked up the warts virus.

I was at an all-time high with my warts when I entered fourth grade. At that time, I had a total of fifty-six warts on my hands. My left pointer finger alone had eighteen warts. Other kids never wanted to sit next to me or play with me and definitely not touch me or my hands.

Adding insult to injury, the teacher I had in this grade was Mrs. Weber, and she never liked me.

I recall very clearly one day we had to turn in our homework and the teacher took it home.

The next day, she returned all the other students' homework and kept mine until the end. Then she announced, in front of the whole class, that she was so disgusted by my exercise/homework book that she felt the need to wash her hands afterward. She said she wouldn't touch it again so I had to get up and take it from her desk. This was a very humiliating experience.

In the meantime, my mother was taking me from one doctor to the next to find a method for removing my warts without having to have surgery. That would have led to severe pain and scarring all over my hands and fingers.

My mother didn't want to put me through this since I'd already went through enough pain physically and emotionally. She wanted to save me from another painful experience with doctors and the medical profession.

She did more research and ultimately found an alternative through a friend of the family. First, she wasn't sure if we should try it but she ultimately took the leap. We had nothing to lose since the only alternative at that time was surgery.

So we drove to Switzerland to a see a spiritual healer.

I remember sitting across from an old man about seventy years old, and he started touching every single one of my warts while he was mumbling something under his breath.

After the session, he told me that in about four to six weeks, my warts would turn brownish in color and I will be able to easily peel them off. It was the beginning of summer and I was off school for about six weeks.

And then the unbelievable happened. After almost three weeks, the warts started to change color and I was able to peel them off one by one.

When I returned to school without any warts on my hands, nobody could believe it.

Oh, and of course, my mother went in to talk to the school board about my teacher, Mrs. Weber, and she sure treated me much nicer after that.

The message I want to bring across with sharing part of my life here is:

When your child is going through a hard or rough time, just be there and love them and listen to what they tell you. That is all they really need. Some children may not dare to speak up because they assume that it will just make it worse.

And as far as medical treatments go, as you can see, nothing is really impossible!

Please never give up and ALWAYS search for alternatives.

You owe this to your child!

I am so grateful for my mother having been there for me and always wrapping her protective wings around me as much as she could, always listening to what I had to say and reading between the lines when she had to.

I am dedicating this to my mother, Jutta E. Wagner, who truly was my hero—she saved me from severe bullying and from unnecessary pain by taking the unconventional route!

I love you, Mom!

Conclusion

So, now that you've read all the chapters, what do you think? Were you cheering along with the stories? Did you shed a tear or two? Children are remarkable. Look at what they overcame. If these children overcame their situations, so can you! Each of the authors shared their story with you with the hope that you keep going in your own life, too.

Whose story resonated most with you? What was in their story that put a spark in you to keep going in your own life? How will you be different from reading their stories? Our goal with this book is to encourage and empower you to keep going in your life—no matter what. It's also our goal to help you in any situation you may be facing with your family. Maybe you also have a daughter who lives with Down syndrome. Or maybe you have a son who lives with autism. Each of these authors are here for you—and so am I. Contact those you feel drawn to and let us know: How can we be of service to you?

Thank you for picking up this book. And if you bought it on Amazon, thank you for helping the children of the Children's Hospital of Eastern Ontario in the Neonatal Intensive Care Unit. You can find more information about this amazing hospital at: **www.cheo.on.ca**

What is one small step you will do today to, *inch by inch*, keep going in your own life?

Inch by Inch

190

Call to Action

Are you an entrepreneur? Do you wish when you were starting out that you'd had some sort of guide book or a collection of stories from entrepreneurs who, *inch by inch*, grew their business to where it is now? Would you like to offer your wisdom in such a guide book?

If so, you can be in the next book anthology, *Inch by Inch: Growing in Business*, compiled by Aime Hutton. Spread your message around the world to those who are thinking of starting a business but are still struggling to find some inspiration from those who have "been there, done that."

Be a part of my next book and share your guidance with new entrepreneurs—the world is waiting for your message!

Contact Aime today!

aime@inchbyinchempowerment.com

The End

CPSIA information can be obtained at www.ICGtesting.com
Printed in the USA
LVOW01s0808070814

397904LV00018B/211/P